SUKKOT

Popular History of Jewish Civilization
General Editor: Raphael Posner

SUKKOT

Compiled by Hayim Halevy Donin

LEON AMIEL PUBLISHER
New York–Paris

Published in the Western Hemisphere by
LEON AMIEL PUBLISHER
New York - Paris

ISBN 8148-0618-x

Printed and bound by Keterpress Enterprises, Jerusalem.
Printed in Israel

CONTENTS

INTRODUCTION

1.   THE SIGNIFICANCE OF SUKKOT   1
The Pilgrim Festival: *The Date – Ḥol ha-Mo'ed – The Last Days – The Most Popular Holiday* – The Festival of Booths: *The Clouds of Glory – Fire and Smoke – Passover in the Sukkah – Symbol of Trust and Faith – Reminder of Poverty – Freedom and Servitude – Inner Freedom* – The Festival of Ingathering: *The Produce of the Land of Israel – The Thanksgiving Holiday – The Thanksgiving Theme in Judaism – The Name Jew – The Gomel Benediction – The Liturgy* – The Festival of Rejoicing: *The Happy Holiday – The Season of Our Rejoicing – Happiness in Judaism – Joy in Worship – Savoring Joy – Rejoice with Jerusalem – The Purpose of Creation – Ḥasidic Emphasis on Happiness – The Most Difficult Mitzvah.*

2.   OTHER SPIRITUAL MOTIFS   19
A Period of Judgment: *Judgment for Water – The Day of Sealing* – Messianic Aspirations: *The Sukkah of David – The Sukkah of Sodom – The Temple and the Sukkah – A Symbol for the Jewish People* – Universalism: *Non-Jews to Observe Sukkot – Praying for the Nations – Sukkah of Leviathan – The Day of the Lord – Symbol of Universal Peace.*

3.   HISTORICAL ASPECTS OF SUKKOT   27
Sukkot After the Exile – Link to Ḥanukkah: *Common Features – Publicizing the Miracle* – Popularity of Four Species: *Symbol of Jewish State – In Synagogues* – Famous Controversies: *Sadducees vs. Pharisees – The Samaritan Way* – Frivolous Fun: *Grabbing Lulavim – Eating Etrogim – Beating Aravot – Hitting Passersby – Splash Parties – Bonfires* – Hakhel – The Commandment to Assemble: *The Great Assembly – The Purpose – Basis of Torah Reading* – When Sukkot is not a Holiday.

4.   THE SUKKAH   40
Rules of Living in Sukkah: *Dispensations – Women and Children – The Special Guests – Hospitality* – Rules of Construction: *The Sekhakh – Thickness – The Walls – Readymade Sukkot – Size – Height* – Decorating the Sukkah: *Emphasis on the Aesthetic – Fruit and Tapestries – At the Conclusion of Yom Kippur – Modern Problems – Competitions.*

5.   THE FOUR SPECIES   50

Hadar — Symbolism of the Four Species: *A Bond with the Earth* — *Four Types of People* — *The Four Limbs* — The Ritual: *The Benediction* — *Solutions to a Dilemma* — *In Temple Times* — *Jerusalem and the Temple Mount* — *The Sabbath* — *The Wavings* — *In All Directions* — *The Procession* — The Etrog: *Selecting the Etrog* — *Experts* — *When Unfit for Use* — *The Etrog Box* — *Borrowing* — *In the Middle Ages* — *The Grafted Etrog* — *Holy Land Etrogim* — Flaws that Invalidate: *The Lulav* — *The Hadassim* — *The Aravot.*

6.   HOSHANA RABBA   68

The Seventh Day of the Willow: *From Moses at Sinai* — The Ritual of the Willow: *The Ceremony* — *The Order* — *Palm-twigs* — The Water Libation Ceremony: *Water-offerings* — *Shiloah* — Rejoicing of the Place of the Water-Drawing: *The Rejoicing* — Hoshana Rabba Customs: *The Serious Aspect* — *The Shadow.*

7.   LITURGICAL ASPECTS OF SUKKOT   76

Kohelet: *Solomon* — *Acceptance into the Canon* — *An Apt Reminder* — The Additional Sukkot Liturgy: *Hoshanot* — *Hallel* — *Ya'aleh ve-Yavo* — Scriptural Readings for Sukkot: *Intermediate Sabbath* — *Shemini Azeret* — Yizkor — Memorial Service: *Charity* — The Prayer for Rain — Tefillin on Hol ha-Mo'ed: *The Benediction* — *Unity.*

8.   SHEMINI AZERET AND SIMHAT TORAH   88

Reasons for the Additional Day: *Parting is Such Sweet Sorrow* — *Universalism and Intimacy* — *The Sukkah on Shemini Azeret* — *Becoming Simhat Torah* — *Solomon's Wisdom* — *The Siyyum* — *The Name* — *The Bridegrooms* — Hakkafot: *Processional Circuits* — *At Weddings* — *The Number* — *The Ritual* — *To the Heights of Ecstasy* — *To the Western Wall* — *Candles in Apples* — *The Second Hakkafot* — Aliyot for Everyone: *"By Permission"* — *"All the Children"* — *Bidding* — *Modern Practice* — Kiddush on Simhat Torah: *My Brother's Simhah* — The Triennial Cycle: *The Haftarah* — *The Transition* — *Evidence from a Church Father* — The Awakening of Russian Jewry.

GLOSSARY
SOURCES
READING LIST

INTRODUCTION

In an age of industrialization and technology, man is becoming further and further removed from his natural surroundings. Without a doubt, the achievements of science in which we so much glory have exacted a price — the increasing alienation of the human being from the world around him, so that the man who operates even the most beneficial of machines can become a mere "button-pusher," a sort of machine himself. Psychologists and sociologists have already sounded the warning as to what this is doing to the inner man; we tend to transfer our machine-directed attitudes to our fellow human beings. The result is that interpersonal relationships become dehumanized. Our appreciation of the enormous complexity of the human being — and the least complex person is infinitely more complex than the most complex machine — is damaged by our constant reliance on technology. Indeed, one of modern Judaism's great theologians, the late Prof. A.J. Heschel, saw the Sabbath as a much-needed withdrawal from the machine world into the human world. Science, industry and technology are also taking a huge price in the irreparable damage they are doing to the world at large. Mankind is just waking up to this challenge, and a new discipline, ecology, studies ways of coping with man's abuse of nature.

Of all the festivals of the Jewish calendar, it is perhaps Sukkot that stresses most the idea of nature. The Jew is commanded to go out and live in natural surroundings for the duration of the festival. Even the city family is obliged to construct a rustic booth and live in it. And for the seven days the believer takes plants in his hand and waves them in all the directions of the compass. Perhaps we can see here the original "flower people." One result of the observance of Sukkot must surely be an increased awareness of the natural world and a very desirable dimunition of man's conceit that he is the master of all.

This is but one of the many motifs of Sukkot. This book explores them all out of the belief that Sukkot, like all the festivals, carries with it a variety of messages which are valid for all time and to all people in whatever circumstances they find themselves. As in the other books of this series, an attempt is made here to give a survey of the history of the festival, its contemporary meaning and relevance, and its laws and customs. This knowledge will contribute to the enjoyment of Sukkot, and make its celebration truly "the season of our rejoicing."

1. THE SIGNIFICANCE OF SUKKOT

The Pilgrim Festival

"The Lord spoke to Moses, saying: Say to the Israelite people: On the fifteenth day of this seventh month there shall be the Festival of Booths to the Lord for seven days."

The Festival of Booths, also known in English as the Festival of Tabernacles, and in Hebrew as *Ḥag ha-Sukkot,* is the third and last of the three major festivals on the Jewish religious calendar, when every male Jew was bidden to make a pilgrimage to Jerusalem, to the place that had been chosen as the site for the central Sanctuary, i.e., Mount Moriah. "Three times a year shall all your males appear before the Lord your God in the place that He will choose. . . ." The first two such festivals are Passover and Shavuot.

Sukkot is observed for seven days, beginning on the fifteenth *The Date* day of the month of Tishrei. It begins two weeks after Rosh

The harvest theme of the Sukkot festival is depicted in this ancient wall painting. Using a sickle and reed basket, ancient Hebrews harvest wheat.
Jews gather in great numbers for worship at the Western Wall during the festival of Sukkot. Almost everyone has his own *lulav* and *etrog.*

Ha-Shanah, the New Year. The first day of the festival (the first two days in the Diaspora) is observed as *yom tov,* a sacred day when no work is permitted. "The first day shall be a sacred occasion; you shall not work at your occupations." This day is observed like the Sabbath in all respects except that work connected with the preparation of food is permitted. This distinction between Sabbath and *yom tov* is based on the biblical directive that: "On the first day, you shall hold a sacred convocation, and on the seventh day a sacred convocation; no work at all shall be done on them; only what every person is to eat, that alone may be prepared for you." *Ḥol ha-Mo'ed*

The remainder of the festival week is called *ḥol ha-mo'ed,* the weekday of the festival. The unique religious duties relating to the Sukkot festival and described further in this book are observed throughout the week. *Ḥol ha-mo'ed* differs from *yom tov* only in that some work may be done on those days.

The Hebrew greeting used on the *yom tov* is *ḥag same'aḥ,* Happy Festival. In Yiddish it is *gut yom tov.* On *ḥol ha-mo'ed, mo'adim le-simḥah* is used in Hebrew; a *guten mo'ed* in Yiddish.

Following the seven days of Sukkot, the Torah calls for the *The Last Days* observance of an additional day of *yom tov* (kept for two days in the Diaspora) on which the distinctive rituals of Sukkot are no longer observed. This day is known both as Shemini Aẓeret, the Eighth Day of Assembly, and as Simḥat Torah, the Rejoicing of the Torah. (In the Diaspora, only the second day of Shemini Aẓeret is called Simḥat Torah). While Shemini Aẓeret-Simḥat Torah possesses an independent religious identity, it has come to be regarded as the concluding *yom tov* day(s) of Sukkot. This feeling is reinforced in the Diaspora where sitting in the *sukkah* is carried over into the first day of Shemini Aẓeret.

In ancient times, Sukkot was regarded as the outstanding *The Most* festival of the year. This is indicated by the fact that in both *Popular* biblical as well as talmudic sources, it is often referred to simply *Holiday* as "The Festival," without mentioning the name. The popularity of Sukkot may have been due to its being celebrated "at the end of the year," when the last of the harvest was gathered in and before a winter period of relative inactivity when the luxury of relaxed rejoicing could be indulged.

Sukkot is a very colorful festival, rich with impressive ceremonies, and filled with many spiritual motifs that relate to religious faith and human character. Sukkot recalls for us the past and teaches us to dream of the future. It is a holiday that breathes the spirit of both nationalism and universalism. The rest of this chapter and the next will explore each of these themes in greater detail.

An 18th-century etching by Jean de Beyer of the Jewish quarter of Amsterdam with *sukkot* along the street.

The Festival of Booths

The most outstanding feature of the Sukkot festival — which also gives the holiday its name — is based on the biblical directive that, for the duration of the festival, the Jewish people is to move out of its permanent dwelling places and move into *sukkot*, "booths," "tabernacles," or "temporary huts."

"You shall live in booths seven days . . . in order that the future generations may know that I made the Israelite people to live in booths when I brought them out of the land of Egypt . . . ." The *sukkah* is thus intended as another reminder of Israel's Exodus from Egypt and to commemorate the divine miracles during the period of Israel's wandering in the desert.

An interesting difference of opinion existed among the sages *The Clouds of* of the Talmud and later Bible commentaries on the question *Glory* whether the *sukkot* referred to in the Bible were actual booths as we know them. Rabbi Akiva held the view that they were set up by the Israelites as a protection against the sun when they camped. But Rabbi Eliezer was of the opinion, possibly question-

In the Sinai desert during the 1973 Yom Kippur War, Israeli soldiers erect a makeshift *sukkah* on top of a half-track, using desert brush for the sides and for the top.

4

Israeli soldiers observe the festival during a momentary respite
on the Golan Heights during the Yom Kippur War.

ing the availability in the desert of vegetation to use for building
the *sukkah*, that the *sukkot* referred to in the biblical passage
were "clouds of glory" which represented the Divine Presence
that protected and guided the Israelites in the desert, and that
the *sukkah* in which we are commanded to sit comes to commemorate that miracle. The *Zohar*, the kabbalistic commentary
on the Torah which tradition attributes to Rabbi Simeon
bar Yoḥai, the talmudic master of the second century, suggests
the same idea. "God linked with Israel seven precious
clouds . . . and Israel crossed the wilderness protected by all of
them. They all form a bond of faith, and therefore Israel was
bidden to live in booths so as to show that it is living in the
shadow of faith."

This was the view that was given primacy by most of the sages and Bible commentaries, some adding that it was these "clouds" that provided protection against the heat and sun. Some pointed to the unusual wording of the biblical passage as lending weight to the view that the biblical *sukkot* were not of the kind made by flesh and blood. Instead of simply saying *ki be-sukkot yashvu*, "in *sukkot* did they live," the biblical phrase is *ki be-sukkot hoshavti* which may mean "I placed them in *sukkot*." Furthermore the association of the word *sukkah* with *ananim* (clouds) is not unusual; it is found elsewhere in the Bible too. Various rational explanations have been sought to explain the biblical references to the "cloud by day and of fire by night"

A festival prayer book, Pisaro, Italy, 1480. The right hand page is the conclusion of the Yom Kippur prayers and the left hand the beginning of the Sukkot services. Note the *sukkah* at the bottom of the page.

as the visible symbol of God's presence. Among them is the attested use of braziers filled with burning wood at the head of the caravans, others point to the smoke that rose from the altar of the burnt offerings as the origin of the representation. The most commonly accepted theory connects the pillars of cloud and fire with the theophany at Sinai, when the descent of the Lord was marked by a thick cloud, by thunder, lightning, smoke and fire.

Another question raised by scholars is why the ritual of the *sukkah* is not observed at the same time of the year as Passover if it was intended as another reminder of the Exodus from Egypt. The answer given is that since people normally sit in *sukkot* for reasons of shade during the spring and summer months, the religious significance of these *sukkot* as testimony to the divine wonders would then be lost. It was therefore set for the seventh month, at the beginning of the rainy season, when it is customary to leave the summer huts to go back into winter homes. To reverse the normal practice is to affirm that Israel is engaged in fulfilling a commandment of the Lord. As a reminder not only of past history, but also of the divine wonders and the miraculous ways of the Lord in protecting Israel at all times, the *sukkah* becomes a symbol of Israel's *bitahon*, trust in God and an expression of its faith that the Holy One, blessed be He, is the source of "our strength and salvation." *Passover in the Sukkah*

The Psalmist expressed that symbolism beautifully: "For in the day of trouble, He will hide me in His *sukkah*; in the shelter of His tabernacle He will conceal me; He will lift me up upon a rock." Sitting in the shade of the *sukkah* became symbolic of Israel sitting in the Divine Presence, under divine protection. That the *sukkah* was a fragile hut only emphasized the lesson that what mattered was the spiritual strength to be found within. *Symbol of Trust and Faith*

Some commentaries saw the fragile *sukkah* as a symbol of poverty. The requirement to move into the *sukkah* in the midst of celebrating the success of the harvest was to humble the po- *Reminder of Poverty* tential arrogance that comes with success and wealth. The *sukkah* teaches a person to remember poverty in the midst of his wealth; to remember the down-trodden in his moment of glory; to remember his simple origin at the time of his elevation to greatness. Thus the *sukkah* was also a means of sensitizing the rich to the needs of the poor and to make them aware of the fragile homes in which the poor live all year round. The Torah itself includes "the Levite, the stranger, the orphan and the widow" among those who are to join a man's household in his festival rejoicing. The 'have-nots' were not to be forgotten.

The concept of Sukkot as a freedom festival is first noted by the *Zohar*. After emphasizing that the *sukkah* symbolizes the shadow of faith in which the Jew lives, it adds that "whoever abides under the shadow of faith acquires freedom for himself and his descendants in perpetuity . . . ." It complements the theme of freedom inherent in the other two pilgrim festivals.

Nations and individuals suffer three kinds of servitude. One is physical, when under the rule or domination of another. Another is spiritual-cultural servitude which occurs when a person or a nation permits the values of a foreign culture to dominate his life or his society, while his own spiritual or cultural values are allowed to deteriorate. The third type of servitude is to the physical lusts which emanate from within man himself, and from which men sometimes cannot escape once they begin to dominate his life. Alcoholism, drugs, promiscuity are examples of the "pleasures" that often wreak havoc with a life. Against these forms of enslavement are arrayed three types of freedom: 1) physical freedom, which for a nation includes political freedom, i.e., independence from foreign rule, 2) spiritual-cultural freedom, the opportunity to live by one's own cultural and spiritual values, and 3) inner freedom, when man is master of himself.

Freedom and Servitude

Passover, when the Israelites were redeemed from Egyptian slavery, celebrates the first of these freedoms. Shavuot, when the

Inner Freedom

Putting up the roof supports of a *sukkah* in Tel Aviv. The *sukkah* walls are made of decorative cloth hangings.

The Ḥasidic Lubavitch group in the United States pioneered a traveling *sukkah* to visit different neighborhoods. They invite people in, encouraging them to fulfill some of the special *mitzvot* of the festival.

Israelites were given the Torah to live by, commemorates the second. Sukkot, in emphasizing discipline and self-restraint in the midst of hearty celebration, comes to symbolize the third freedom.

The Festival of Ingathering

The agricultural aspect of Sukkot is reflected by still another name the Bible uses when referring to this holiday: *Ḥag ha-Asif*, the "Festival of Ingathering." The time of its observance is set "at the end of the year when you gather in the results of your work from the field." The Bible thus takes into account the normal inclination of an agricultural society to celebrate anyway at this time of the year and exploits the occasion to re-emphasize

9

the spiritual and national-historic lessons derived from two interlocking themes emphasized by the Bible and crucial to Jewish thought and doctrine: namely, the historical experience of the Exodus from Egypt and the spiritual motif of divine protection.

In fact, all of the three pilgrim festivals reflect an agricultural theme, being tied to the produce of the Land of Israel. Passover, marked the early harvesting of the barley, commemorated by the special offering of the *Omer* on the second day of the festival. Shavuot marked the harvesting of the wheat, the last grain harvest of the season, and the beginning of the fruit harvest. The ceremony of bringing the "first fruits" to the Temple as an offering of thanksgiving was a major feature of its celebration. And Sukkot was fixed to coincide with the final harvest of the year, "after the ingathering from your threshing floor and your wine press" before the rainy season and the winter months set in. Maimonides, the outstanding rabbinic authority of the 12th century, notes that the reason for the festival at this time of the year is precisely because it is a time of rest, and men are free from pressing labors. *The Produce of the Land of Israel*

The essence and most important aspect of the agricultural motif is as a holiday of thanksgiving for the Land of Israel and its produce. Bible commentaries note that "Sukkot comes particularly for rejoicing and thanksgiving for the storehouses filled with the ingathered crops of the field and the harvested fruit of the tree." According to Isaac Abrabanel, the 15th century statesman and philosopher who was also an important Bible commentator, each of the three festivals reflects a different aspect of God's lovingkindness for which thanksgiving is in order: 1) Passover for freeing Israel from Egyptian slavery; 2) Shavuot, for granting Israel the Torah; and 3) Sukkot, for the inheritance of the Land of Israel. *The Thanksgiving Holiday*

The theme of a thanksgiving that relates to the final harvest was the inspiration for the Bible-reading Pilgrim Fathers who came to America to similarly declare a Thanksgiving Day.

The quality of gratitude and thankfulness is indeed one of *The Thanks-* the basic virtues that Judaism encourages in man. Actually *giving Theme in* thanksgiving serves as another way of affirming one's faith in the *Judaism* Master of the Universe, since the manifestation of such a feeling implies a concommitant belief that there is Someone to whom to give thanks. On the other hand, ingratitude is viewed as a heresy. When the Prophets castigated Israel for its sins against God, they phrased the condemnation in terms of Israel's ingratitude. There is no more grievous sin against God — and perhaps also against man.

The very name Jew in its Hebrew form is derived from and is *The Name Jew* synonymous with the Hebrew word for thanksgiving. The Bible says that when Leah gave birth to her fourth son, "she said: 'This time I will thank the Lord,' therefore she named him Judah" (Hebrew for 'thanks to the Lord'). Jew is a contraction of Judah or Judean, which name came to be applied to all of the Israelites after ten of the tribes of Israel were carried off into Babylonian captivity in the eighth century b.c.e., and only the descendants of the Kingdom of Judah survived.

The Psalmist regarded the ability to be thankful as a good thing for man: "It is a good thing to give thanks to the Lord and to sing praises unto Thy name, O Most High." Shakespeare phrased it poignantly: "Beggar that I am, I am even poor in thanks." There is indeed none so poor as he who is incapable of thanksgiving.

And so Judaism prescribes blessings for all occasions, from *The Gomel* the most routine to the most rare. Though not all blessings are in *Benediction* the form of thanksgiving — some are exclusively in praise of God — they all serve to remind man of God's Sovereignty over the world and to place man's humble role into proper perspective.

Although the Talmud says, "Four are required to give thanks," basing itself on the instances enumerated in Psalm 107, Judaism teaches that whenever one is delivered from any danger, it is appropriate to recite a blessing of thanksgiving. That blessing is known as *gomel (bentchen gomel)*: "Blessed art Thou, O Lord our God, King of the Universe, Who does good to the undeserving, and has dealt kindly with me."

During the 1948-49 War of Independence, members of Kibbutz Sa'ad conduct Sukkot services near trenches surrounding the kibbutz.

Prayers of thanksgiving are part of daily Jewish liturgy. The *The Liturgy* next to the last blessing of the *Amidah*, said three times every day of the year and four times on Sabbaths and festivals, begins with the words: *Modim anahnu lakh*: "We give thanks unto Thee, for Thou art the Lord our God and the God of our fathers for ever and ever. . . We will give thanks unto Thee and declare Thy praise for our lives which are committed to Thy hand. . . ." The very young child is taught to say a simple and beautiful prayer of thanksgiving upon arising each morning: "*Modeh ani*, I thank Thee O King Who lives for always and Who, as I awaken, returned my soul to me in mercy; we can ever trust in Thee." Nevertheless, Jewish liturgists recognized that there exists a gap between the thanks that rightly ought to be expressed and man's ability to properly do so. That inability is summed up in one of the most beautiful liturgical passages recited every Sabbath and festival morning:

> Were our mouths full of song as the sea,
> And our tongues of exultation as the multitude of its waves;
> And our lips of praise as the wide-extended skies;
> Were our eyes shining with light like the sun and the moon,
> And our hands were spread forth like the eagles of the air,
> And our feet were swift as the wild deer,
> We should still be unable to thank Thee and to bless Thy
>   Name, O Lord our God . . . .

During the 1973 Yom Kippur war, on the eve of the Sukkot festival, an Israeli soldier, carrying his Four Species, is waiting for a lift on the Tel Aviv - Jerusalem road.

So that while no day of the year passes without this spiritual motif, and no festival is without it, the Sukkot celebration carries the theme of thanksgiving to new heights.

The Festival of Rejoicing

An often overlooked but essential ingredient in the philosophy of Judaism highlighted by Sukkot is *simhah*, happiness, gladness, or joy. While it is a religious duty to rejoice on all the festivals, nowhere is happiness emphasized as much as it is on Sukkot.

The word *simhah* does not at all appear in the Bible in con- *The Happy* nection with the Passover celebration and only once in connec- *Holiday* tion with Shavuot. In connection with Sukkot, it is mentioned three times: "You shall rejoice before the Lord your God seven days"; "You shall rejoice in your festival . . ."; "You shall have nothing but joy."

The liturgy specifically designates this festival as *zeman* *The Season of* *simhateinu*, the "season of our rejoicing," a reflection of the *Our Rejoicing* extra measure of happiness attached to this holiday. According to Maimonides, happiness parallels the mood of thanksgiving upon completion of the agricultural labors of the year, and is the very purpose of the festival. But instead of undisciplined frivolity and wild excesses, the expression of this happiness is directed towards God. The happiness is sanctified.

Even a cursory glance elsewhere in Jewish sources reveals the *Happiness in* really central role that *simhah* plays in Jewish thought, not only *Judaism* on Sukkot but throughout the year, and in all of man's activities.

The Almighty found fault with Israel "because you did not serve the Lord your God *be-simhah*, in joy and gladness." God's complaint was not that Israel ceased to worship Him, but that the quality of happiness and gladness was lacking in their worship.

That *simhah* is regarded as an essential ingredient in the worship of God is derived also from other sources: The Psalmist says: "Serve the Lord with gladness"; "Let the righteous be glad, let them exult before God; let them rejoice with gladness." The ingredient of happiness in worship was to be reflected both in song as well as in the person's mood and emotional feeling.

The Talmud emphasizes that the Divine Presence manifests itself only on a joyous heart, and when there is joy in fulfilling the divine commandment. "The *Shekhinah* (Divine Presence) rests upon man neither in indolence nor in gloom, nor in frivolity, nor in levity, nor in vain pursuits, but only in rejoicing connected with a religious act."

Not only should worship be accompanied by a feeling of gladness but also the performance of all the ritual and ethical commandments. For happiness in worship and in the performance of other religious duties is indicative of love for God. As when a person loves another, he cheerfully and gladly fulfills the beloved's requests. The mere opportunity to do so brings joy to the heart; indeed the mere presence of a loved one is a source of gladness. If there is true love of God, it must therefore reflect itself in joy and gladness. If the religious duty that is performed is done only in a perfunctory way, it is nothing less than an indication of the absence of love for God.

To allow for full expression of this sense of happiness, Jewish religious life provides many opportunities for feasting and merry-making, for song and cheer, for dance and music. Not only are the festivals occasion for rejoicing but so also are the ceremonies of *brit* (circumcision), *pidyon ha-ben* (redemption of the first-born), *bar-mitzvah*, wedding, and the ceremony of completing a talmudic tractate. These are all events when an accompanying meal is religiously mandatory and the celebration is a religious duty.

The joyous zeal evident at traditional Jewish weddings (the more religious the gathering, the greater the sense of ecstasy) is not just a cultural happenstance. It is in response to the talmudic teaching that it is proper to dance before the bride, to entertain her and gladden her heart. And as one dances before the bride and groom, so does one dance before the Lord on Simḥat Torah, at the *Simḥat Bet ha-Sho'evah*, and on other religious occasions.

Savoring Joy

The sages lost no opportunity to emphasize rejoicing. "When the month of Adar enters, rejoicing is increased." To enjoy the full gladness merited by each occasion, the overlapping of joyous occasions was proscribed: "One rejoicing may not be merged in another rejoicing." This is the reason why weddings are not performed on the Intermediate Days of Sukkot and Passover. The joy of the festival and of the wedding each deserves its own full expression without being diluted with the joy of the other.

Rejoice with Jerusalem

Except for one verse that speaks of requesting (i.e., praying for) the peace of Jerusalem, Jews are bidden to be happy with and rejoice over Jerusalem. Not somber prayer, but gladness and joy is what is demanded by the Prophets: "Rejoice with Jerusalem, and be glad for her, all you who love her." The Jewish pledge of allegiance to Jerusalem is in terms of making Jerusalem the major source of its happiness, affording it the greatest joy; ". . . If I set not Jerusalem above my chiefest joy." The degree to which sanctity and holiness goes with happiness and not with sadness, with joy and not with somberness is reflected by the identification of Jerusalem, the holiest city in the world, with the verse "The joy of the whole earth," the core of the earth's joy. While it is well known that all cemetery areas and burial plots were located outside Jerusalem's city limits, so that the impurity of death should not impinge on the sanctity of the city, it is not so well known that sadness itself was similarly regarded as sacreligious to the atmosphere of Jerusalem's sanctity.

The Purpose of Creation

One of the sages even ventured the idea that the sole purpose of creation was to make possible song and melody in life. The presence of joy is thus to be considered as the peak of creation and an integral part of natural man.

And while the sages understood that *simḥah* requires the delight of the senses, "there is no rejoicing except it include food and drink," which adds to cheer and lightheartedness, yet the essence of joy cannot be based exclusively on such pleasure. Maimonides stressed that a balance be struck. If Judaism emphasizes happiness, it is not as a goal to be pursued but as a means through which the highest spiritual existence can be attained.

During the past few centuries, it was ḥasidic Jewry that most *Hasidic* contributed to restoring the spirit of happiness in Jewish worship *Emphasis on* and in Jewish ritual to its rightful place. It was they who re- *Happiness* introduced song and melody, dance and celebration in reaching out to God, an approach that has since left its impact on all other elements in Jewry. Ḥasidism taught that joy is the gift of God to those who revere Him, and that true joy is to be found exclusively in the spiritual domain.

More than all the others, Ḥasidism disparaged sadness, considering it an evil tantamount to idol worship. If the Talmud taught that God's presence comes to rest only on a happy heart, then obviously God does not dwell where there is sadness. Ḥasidism in fact emphasized the basic superiority of happiness of the spirit at all times as a characteristic of day to day living and in all interpersonal relations. It drew upon the wellsprings of Jewish faith in the midst of intolerable physical conditions to re-emphasize the joy in life, the happiness which comes essentially from within, not without.

An 18th century poet, Nathaniel Cotton also put it beautifully:

> If solid happiness we prize
> Within our breasts this jewel lies,
> And they are fools who roam
> The world has nothing to bestow
> From our own selves, our joys must flow. . . .

The Biblical commandments that "You shall have nothing *The Most* but joy" and "You shall rejoice before the Lord your *Difficult* God . . ."may on the surface seem easy to fulfill. Yet when one *Mitzvah*

A *sukkah* decoration from Morocco, 1954. The sentence in the circle reads: "O Lord, spread over us a *sukkah* of peace." Pinḥas the son of Aaron, is added to the traditional *ushpizin* presumably for symmetry.

great sage was asked "Which is the most difficult *mitzvah* of the Torah to observe," he replied that the *mitzvah* of "rejoicing on the festival" was the most difficult. The commandment requires Jews to be happy and cheerful throughout the eight days, and while human beings can obey commandments that require doing, they cannot, even with the best intentions, always respond to commandments requiring certain feelings or emotions. Yet the capacity of the Jew to express happiness under the most trying circumstances was described by the noted author Elie Wiesel: "Those Jews [of Auschwitz], who on their journey to the end of all hope managed to dance on Simḥat Torah; the Jews who studied pages of the Talmud, without having the books before them, as they carried heavy rocks on their shoulders; the Jews who sang Sabbath songs to themselves as they were being worked to death — they have taught us how a Jew is supposed to behave in time of trouble. For them, the commandment 'Rejoice on your festival' was an impossible commandment to observe — but observe it they did."

2. OTHER SPIRITUAL MOTIFS

A Period of Judgment

The initial inclination — based on Scripture — is to contrast the festive nature of Sukkot with the solemn mood of the High Holy Day period which immediately precedes it. Rosh Ha-Shanah and Yom Kippur are days of judgment; Sukkot is a period of rejoicing. The latter balances the "affliction of the soul" required on Yom Kippur. Commentaries take note of the spiritual significance of the relationship: that the rejoicing is a reflection of the confidence felt in having merited full atonement on Yom Kippur. Some even see the same significance in the Four Species: "Israel received the Four Species as a palm of victory to hold aloft and publicly proclaim that the Jewish people had emerged victoriously from the divine judgment of Rosh Ha-Shanah and Yom Kippur."

Yet in the course of time, Sukkot came to be regarded as an extension of the period of repentance. The period of judgment which began with Rosh Ha-Shanah was extended to include Sukkot. The talmudic sages expressed the belief that the world is judged at four different periods of the year: "On Passover, for grain; on Shavuot, for the fruit of the trees; on the New Year all the inhabitants of the world pass before Him, like flocks of sheep . . . .; and on the Festival [Sukkot] they are judged for water."

As the judgment period for water, Sukkot became the most appropriate time to concentrate on prayers for water. It must be remembered that the period of rain in Israel begins at just about the time of Sukkot and there was widespread concern for an adequate rainfall. Many of the rituals to be described later in this book, particularly the Water-Libation ceremony in the Temple, and the ritual of the *aravah* were rituals of request for rain. Some even saw this theme reflected in the waving-ritual that was performed with the *lulav* and *etrog*. Certainly water was a major theme of the *piyyutim*, the special liturgical poems recited throughout Sukkot. The seventh and last day of Sukkot, which became known as Hoshana Rabba was the day on which the judgment was sealed. The Temple ritual on this day reached a climax in the prayers for water.

Since the life and well-being of man is so totally dependent on water, it was not long before Hoshana Rabba, the day of judgment for water, came to be regarded as the final day on which man's fate is also sealed. References in rabbinic literature identifying "the day of the *aravah*" as the *yom ha-ḥitum*, the Day of the Sealing, reflects its development as an extension of Yom Kippur.

The *Zohar* has it that "the seventh day of the festival marks the conclusion of the judgment of the world;" and later rabbinic literature reaffirms that "the day of the *aravah* is the day on which the judgment is sealed."

Since the traditional belief is that "on Rosh Ha-Shanah it [God's judgment] is written, and on Yom Kippur it is sealed," Hoshana Rabba was explained as the day when the decrees sealed on Yom Kippur were confirmed. Somehow, repentance and a suspension of any evil decrees was still possible through Hoshana Rabba. This explains why the greeting of *gemar tov*, "be sealed for good," said from Rosh Ha-Shanah through Yom Kippur, is actually in popular use through the seventh day of Sukkot.

This transformation of Hoshana Rabba from another joyous, festive day into a solemn day of judgment, first for water, then also of man, gave it a special importance giving rise to a number of distinct customs that grew up around this day. These will be discussed in Chapter Five.

Since it is not only Israel but all the world that is affected by whether or not the coming year is blessed with rain or cursed with drought, the judgment motif that runs through Sukkot became related also to the messianic and universal aspects of the festival.

Messianic Aspirations

In the period following the destruction of the First Temple (586 b.c.e.) the humble *sukkah* came to symbolize the national home that had been laid waste, thus relating the *sukkah* to the people's longing for the re-establishment of the Temple and of their national sovereignty. The Prophet Amos gives expression to this longing and to this symbolism of the *sukkah* when in a vision of the messianic era at "the end of days," he says: "In that day will I raise up the tabernacle (*sukkah*) of David that is fallen, and I will raise up his ruins, and I will build it as in the days of old." An ancient Aramaic translation renders it as: "I will raise up the *kingdom* of the fallen House of David." Based on this verse in Amos, the following short prayer was inserted into the Grace

The Sukkah of David

21

after Meals during the Intermediate Days of the festival: "May the All Merciful One raise up for us the fallen tabernacle of David." It was this prayer that primarily influenced the masses in all succeeding generations to see in the *sukkah* the symbol of the destroyed Temple and of the fallen kingdom.

Seen in these terms, several midrashic passages become clearer. One passage says: "All who fulfill the *mitzvah* of *sukkah* in this world, the Holy One blessed be He will place him in the *sukkah* of Sodom in the future to come." This perplexing Midrash is generally explained on the basis of the prophetic view that in the messianic period Sodom will be spiritually and physically rehabilitated and all of Israel will share in its restored beauty. The *sukkah* of Sodom is thus promised as the messianic reward for keeping the ritual of *sukkah*. But the passage becomes even clearer if the four letters that make up the word for Sodom, i.e., *S,D,O,M,* are not understood as a word which spells out Sodom, but as an abbreviation for: *The Sukkah of Sodom*

Sukkat *David* Malkenu; the *sukkah* of David our King; or
Sukkat *David* U'melech *Mashiaḥ*, the *sukkah* of David and
    King Messiah; or
Sukkat *David* Mukemet; the raised tabernacle of David.

The association of the *sukkah* with the Temple explains the custom that grew up in some Jewish communities, particularly Eastern, to use no nails in its construction. Undoubtedly, the custom is an extension of the biblical commandment to build an altar of stone, without using any metal tools. Since metal is the instrument of war it was not to come in contact with the altar, the symbol of peace. In the popular mind, the construction of the *sukkah* was to be subjected to the same restriction. *The Temple and the Sukkah*

From the altar and the Temple, the symbolism of the *sukkah* was easily extended to symbolize the downtrodden existence of the whole House of Israel, and much popular Jewish literature of *A Symbol for the Jewish People* the Middle Ages and the modern period makes use of this association.

One poem describes a father building a tiny *sukkah* from thin poles, covering it with loose *sekhakh* and yet sitting in it in comfort. The second stanza continues to describe a pale, crying child complaining of the winds rushing through the *sukkah*, conspiring to destroy it. The response of the father in the concluding third stanza reflects an optimism for the nation's future. Though storms rage about and the winds blow through, and within it sit people who may become frightened and disillusioned, this fragile-appearing *sukkah* remains standing strong to survive forever.

Another popular Yiddish folk song that sees the *sukkah* as the symbol of Zion, the House of David, the whole House of Israel, carries the refrain:

> Mother, you will yet be redeemed
> The *sukkah* will yet be rebuilt.

Universalism

Parallel to the messianic motif and its theme of Israel's redemption, Sukkot also reflects a distinctive universalism. In contrast to

Building and decorating a *sukkah* is usually a family project. This Tel Aviv family seems to be enjoying it.

23

all the other Jewish festivals which were designed to express the singularity and distinctiveness of the Jewish people and to emphasize the special intimate bond that God created with Israel, Sukkot was also given a universal character in addition to these intimate national characteristics.

While nowhere do we find the Hebrew prophets calling upon *Non-Jews to* the gentile world to observe any of the Jewish festivals, this is *Observe Sukkot* not so with Sukkot. The Prophet Zechariah, in his vision of the messianic era, prophesied that in the end of days, "it shall come to pass that every one that is left of all nations that came up against Jerusalem shall go up from year to year to worship the King, the Lord of Hosts, and to keep the Feast of Booths."

While according to Jewish teaching, the non-Jewish world is obligated only to observe the Seven Commandments of the Children of Noah, the non-observance of Sukkot by the gentile word is seen by the Prophet as a "sin," a spiritual failure. Midrashic literature in fact regards the *mitzvah* of *sukkah* as the test that will be given gentiles to determine the sincerity of their faith in the One God.

Evidence for the universalism of Sukkot is seen in the very *Praying for the* order of the sacrifices prescribed by the Bible and performed in *Nations* the ancient Temple. They differ noticeably for Sukkot. While on the other festivals, notably Passover, the number of sacrificial offerings did not change from day to day, on Sukkot there was not only a doubling of all the offerings, but the bulls for the burnt offering were brought in declining number — so that the sum brought on the seven days added up to seventy.

"To what do those seventy bulls correspond?" asked the Talmud. And they answered, "To the seventy nations." As tradition saw the entire world consisting of seventy nations, these sacrifices were regarded as atonement offerings by Israel on behalf of all the world.

The mystical essence of the *sukkah* is captured in still another version of the same midrashic passage mentioned earlier, which says: "All who fulfill the *mitzvah* of *sukkah* in this world, the Holy One blessed be He will grant him a share in the *sukkah* of Leviathan in the future to come."

וְשׁוֹר הַבָּר   לִוְיָתָן

The Leviathan depicted with the *shor ha-bar* ("the wild ox") in a folk-art picture from Poland, 19th century. These two mythical animals will be served at the banquet for the righteous in the world to come.

Leviathan is the term generally applied in midrashic literature to the largest sea animal. It parallels the use of the word *behemoth* as the name for the largest land animal. Yet neither name, says Samson Raphael Hirsch (1808-1888), actually applies to a specific creature, but is symbolic of all living creatures on land and in the sea. In this vein he understands the verse from Isaiah: "In that day the Lord ... will punish Leviathan the elus-

Sukkah of Leviathan

25

ive serpent, Leviathan the twisting serpent, and He will slay the dragon of the sea." Since animals are often used by the Prophets to symbolize different nations, the serpents are understood to be various forces in mankind. The Leviathan is symbolic of human kingdoms, of social orders. Hirsch draws the conclusion that the phrase "*sukkah* of Leviathan in the future" is the symbol of collective mankind, of the tabernacle that encompasses a united world.

Hirsch finds support for this interpretation by an analysis of the Hebrew word *leviatan*. He concludes that it is derived from the Hebrew root *l'v'h* which means "to be joined together," thus signifying a social bond, or a social organization.

Hirsch interprets Isaiah as prophesying that the path of mankind as it approaches the messianic era will lead to the destruction of those powers who pursue their aims by either aggression, force or deceit. This will be followed by a universal recognition and praise of God by those who survive the destruction. Their annual pilgrimage to Jerusalem to celebrate the festival of Sukkot as described in Zechariah 14:15 is symbolic of the fact that all the world will come under the shadow of the *sukkah*, namely, within the protection of God's lovingkindness. This is the meaning of the *sukkah* of Leviathan and of the prayer said on the last day of Sukkot, when the Jew takes leave of the *sukkah* to return to his permanent abode: "May it be Thy will, Lord our God and God of our fathers, that just as I have observed and sat in the *sukkah* so may I be privileged to dwell in the *sukkah* made of the hide of Leviathan." It is a prayer for the "day to come" period of the messianic era when "the Lord shall be King over all the earth." The *sukkah* emerges also as a symbol of universal peace. A daily reminder of that is found in the daily evening service, where in the *hashkivenu* benediction, the following prayer is found, "And spread over us Thy tabernacle of peace."

While the identification of the *sukkah* as a national symbol remained uppermost in the minds of the Jewish people, the universal aspect was reflected in the prayer designed to be said whenever entering the *sukkah* and when finally taking leave of it: "May it be Thy will . . . that the Divine Presence dwell among us, and spread over us the tabernacle of peace by virtue of our observance of the *mitzvah* of *sukkah*."

3.   HISTORICAL ASPECTS OF SUKKOT

The biblical Book of Nehemiah, after describing how the Torah was taught to the Jewish exiles who had returned from Babylonia to Palestine at the end of the sixth century b.c.e., tells that they then proceeded to build *sukkot* in order to properly keep the festival. "And all the congregation of them that came back out of captivity made booths, and dwelt in booths, for since the days of Joshua the son of Nun unto that day had not the children of Israel done so." From this passage it appears that since the days of Joshua, the Israelites had not kept the ritual of the *sukkah*, and that the practice was reinstituted in the days of Ezra and Nehemiah. That it had been ignored during the 70-odd years of the exile is probably so, but scholars find it hard to literally accept the statement that it had been ignored since Joshua. They point to Ezra 3:4 and earlier Books of the Bible that indicate a major awareness of Sukkot and of its great popularity. And so the verse in Nehemiah is interpreted as a way of saying "that a Sukkot like this one the Israelites did not celebrate all the years in its memory."

It would however appear from Nehemiah that three of the Four Species were used to cover the *sukkah*. "Go forth unto the mount and fetch olive branches, and branches of wild olive, and myrtle branches and palm branches, and branches of thick trees, to make booths. . . ." There is no mention made of the willow nor any indication from the verses in Nehemiah as to whether the Four Species (see page 32) were also taken separately.

Sukkot After the Exile

27

A coin from the Bar Kokhba
period, dated 134/135 c.e.
showing the Four Species.
An Israeli child puts the
finishing touches to a
lavishly decorated *sukkah*.

Link to Ḥanukkah

There is no doubt however that the use of the Four Species as a separate ritual was well established and popular during the period of the Hasmoneans, after 165 b.c.e. The Book of Maccabees tells how the Hasmoneans even used the *lulav* and *etrog* when rededicating the Temple they had reconquered from the pagan Assyrian Greeks. As they had been unable to observe this ritual at its proper time during Sukkot on account of the war, they made it part of the Ḥanukkah celebration. As a matter of fact, Maccabees II clearly states that the entire Ḥanukkah dedication was patterned after Sukkot. The eight days were celebrated "with gladness, like the Feast of Booths" which, together with Shemini Aẓeret, is an eight day holiday. And in letters then sent by the Jews of Palestine to the Jews of Egypt, the latter were requested to observe the decision of the Maccabean *bet din* to make "the Sukkot festival on the 25th of Kislev" (the date of Ḥanukkah).

The connection between the two festivals is reflected in some common features: both are observed for eight days; on both holidays the full *Hallel* is recited throughout the week; the Torah reading is parallel insofar as each consists of an account of offerings brought on each of the respective days. *Common Features*

There are also two halakhic disputes in the Talmud that give evidence of the original relationship between Sukkot and Ḥanukkah. One reason for the School of Shammai's view that the Ḥanukkah lights are to be lit in decreasing order, i.e., beginning with eight candles on the first night and diminishing gradually to one, is to "symbolize the bullock offerings of the festival," which are also brought in decreasing order. The festival referred to in the passage is Sukkot as the only offerings that follow this procedure were those brought on Sukkot, as described in Numbers 29.

Another dispute between Rabbi Judah and the Sages revolves around damages and the question of responsibility in the case of a shopkeeper who placed his Ḥanukkah lights outside his shop in

A carved bone plaque from the
Byzantine period (330-640 c.e.),
found near Beisan. It shows Jewish
symbols all reminiscent of the Temple:
a *menorah*, a *lulav*, an *etrog* and an
incense shovel.

Stone relief from the synagogue at Ostia, Italy, first through
fourth century, shows a *lulav* and *etrog* to the left of the
menorah and a *shofar* to the right.

the public domain and it caused damage. The same dispute is
recorded in the Jerusalem Talmud, where a parallel case is introduced as precedent: that of a shopkeeper who builds a *sukkah*
outside his shop and which causes damage to a passerby.

It is apparent from the latter talmudic dispute that it was also *Publicizing the*
the practice to build *sukkot* on the public streets, though the *Miracle*
authoritative practice was to do so only in the private domain. It
is conjectured that this custom started with the Maccabees, who
did so in order to publicize the miracle of their victory. The
practice was retained in the rules governing the kindling of the

30

Ḥanukkah lights, which is also to be done in a way that publicly proclaims the miracle.

The association of Ḥanukkah with Sukkot recalls the fact that the first Temple, built by King Solomon on Mount Moriah in Jerusalem, was consecrated and dedicated during Sukkot.

Popularity of Four Species

There is evidence to indicate that during the Hadrianic persecutions and the Bar Kokhba period (circa 135 c.e.) great effort was made by Bar Kokhba and his soldiers to obtain sets of the Four Species and observe this religious duty even during their military campaigns. The Midrash mentions the Four Species together with circumcision, the study of Torah, and the eating of *mazzah* as among the religious observances for which the Jews were prepared to struggle and die for in the face of anti-religious decrees.

So widespread was the use of the Four Species, that they *Symbol of* became the symbol of the revived Jewish state, taking their place *Jewish State* alongside the *menorah*, the *shofar* and the Ark of the Law. On the half-shekel coin issued by Simeon, the Hasmonean, there appears on one side the relief of an *etrog* between two *lulavim*. The quarter-shekel coin has on one side a relief of two *lulavim*, bound with myrtles and willows, and on the other side an *etrog* with the *pitom* pointing upwards. Coins from the Bar Kokhba period, during the second century of the common era, also show a *lulav* with an *etrog* at its left.

The popular use of the *lulav* and *etrog* as a Jewish symbol *In Synagogues* continued for many centuries, both in Israel and in the Diaspora. They are to be found as decorations engraved on ritual items and on floor mosaics of ancient synagogues. Such mosaics were found in a fifth century synagogue on Mount Carmel and in a sixth century synagogue in Beit Alfa. An old mosque in Gaza, built over an ancient synagogue, contains a stone showing an *etrog* and *lulav* at the side of a *menorah*. Inside Jewish sepulchers in the

Roman catacombs, dating back to the second through the fourth centuries, were found *Kiddush* cups that had the Four Species engraved on them.

It is therefore not surprising to find mention of Sukkot even in the New Testament, nor to find that the early Christians adopted the *lulav*, the palm branch, as the central rite of the Sunday before Easter (Palm Sunday) as an adaptation of the carrying of flowers in the early spring which was a popular rite in the Greek and Roman world.

Famous Controversies

Sukkot was the focal point of a great historical controversy between the Sadducees and the Pharisees. It centered on the people's belief that Sukkot was a judgment period for water and on the two ritual ceremonies related to it: 1) the water-libation ritual and 2) the ritual of the willows (see pages 69-72). Since there is no basis in Scripture either for the belief or for the rituals, the Sadducee ruler who accepted only the authority of the Written Torah and rejected the validity and authority of the Oral Law, refused to perform them. It is told that on one occasion the Sadducean High Priest, said to be none other than King Alexander Yannai (2nd century b.c.e.) who also held the priestly position, showed his contempt for the tradition by pouring the water not on the altar but on his feet. This so aroused the anger of the celebrants gathered in the Temple courtyard that they pelted him with their *etrogim*. The Sadducean interpretation of Scripture also led them to use the Four Species as a covering for their booths and not as a separate ritual. It may also be noted that the Samaritans place their palm branches on a net roof of the *sukkah*, put interwoven twigs on the palm branches, hang citrus fruit and also willow branches from the net roof supported by four poles. (The Samaritan sect, which traces its ancestry to those who settled in Samaria after the Ten Tribes were taken into captivity in the year 722 b.c.e., adopted many

Sadducees vs. Pharisees

The Samaritan Way

A 4th-5th century c.e. bronze oil lamp from Alexandria.
The *menorah* handle is flanked by a *lulav* and *etrog*
on one side and a *shofar* on the other side.

Jewish practices. They affirmed their faith in the Five Books of
Moses and to this day observe rites contained in Scripture.)

The Arab riots that plagued the Samaritans during various
periods forced them to build their *sukkot* inside their homes, and
over hundreds of years, this had become a tradition.

Frivolous Fun

Jewish literature records a series of festival pranks that became
customary during Sukkot. While these may have long ago dis-

appeared, traces of these customs are to be found in some of the more frivolous antics that still take place in the synagogues on Simḥat Torah and on the streets of Israel on such holidays as Purim and Yom ha-Aẓma'ut.

The Mishnah records that when the first day of the festival fell on a Sabbath, the people would leave their *lulavim* and *etrogim* with the *ḥazzanim* (the position was equivalent to that of today's sexton) on the day before so as not to desecrate the Sabbath by carrying. On the morrow the *ḥazzanim* would throw *Grabbing* out these *lulavim* to the crowd who came to collect them. As *Lulavim* the people grabbed at the *lulavim*, they proceeded to beat one another with them. The *bet din* became concerned about the physical danger involved and ruled that the Four Species were no longer to be brought to the Temple for Sabbath use.

A further Mishnah tells of a prank that used to take place on the seventh day of Sukkot when the ritual need of *etrogim* was over. Adults would grab the *lulavim* away from the children and eat their *etrogim*. The Rashi commentary notes that this did not *Eating Etrogim* violate the prohibition of stealing, because the custom was prac-

A lithograph showing various Sukkot scenes from an early 18th century book on Jewish Ceremonials written by a non-Jew, Paul Christian Kirchner, published in Nuremberg, Germany.

a) Two *sukkot* built into the garrets of two houses. Note the swing-open roof on the one to the right, and the presence of beds or couches in both.

b) Father and son performing the 'wavings' of the *lulav*. Kirchner explained the scene as a chasing away of the evil spirits.

c) Reciting a blessing over the food.

d) Meal in the *sukkah*.

e) Beating the leaves off a willow branch, a ritual performed on Hoshana Rabba.

f) Scene showing the branches being burned after Sukkot. The building beyond it is probably the synagogue. The spire makes it the tallest building which conforms to traditional requirements.

ticed as a form of rejoicing. Although the Tosafot commentary
interprets the words of the Mishnah to mean that the children
themselves would throw away their *lulavim* and eat their *etrogim*,
it makes reference to a parallel prank that was apparently practiced at weddings: young men, riding towards the groom on
horseback, would fight with one another, tear at each other's
clothes or damage the other's horse and that it was all done in
the name of rejoicing.

Decorating the *sukkah* in Alsace; the women are doing
the work under the supervision of the master of the
house. An etching by Alphons Levi.

There is even a view that the inexplicable custom of beating
the *aravot* on the side of the altar, described in the Mishnah just
before its description of the frivolous pranks, was also a form of
fun engaged in by the people as part of their rejoicing. Babylonian Jewry apparently regarded the beating of the *aravot* in this
context, for they refused to do it in the synagogue, not willing to
engage there in such frivolity. They instead went outside to the
synagogue courtyard to beat their *aravot*.

36

The custom of "throwing" and "grabbing" next found expression in the practice, recorded by Rabbi Jacob Moellin in the 14th century, "of women throwing fruit on the children on Simḥat Torah." Another 14th century source records the custom in some places that the *Hatan-Torah* (see page 94) would distribute (i.e., throw) nuts and apples to the congregation who would gather (i.e., grab) them up.

In Kurdistan, it was the custom of children to take strong *Hitting* palm leaves and hit passers-by with them. While in Tripolitania, it *Passersby* was customary for adults on Hoshana Rabba to slap their friends' back with the *aravot*; in Europe the *aravot* were treated with dignity and were thrown to the top of the Holy Ark. The latter too must have been a form of frivolous activity, for Babylonian Jewry did not follow that custom but took their *aravot* home.

During the Middle Ages, there rose the prank of throwing *Splash Parties* water on one another and throwing people, fully clothed in their festival outfits, into nearby lakes and streams.

The Sukkot pranks reached their peak in some European *Bonfires* communities where on Simḥat Torah people would take their *sukkot* apart and light bonfires with them and dance and sing around the fires. Many rabbinic authorities objected to this practice on halakhic grounds, but others defended it. The danger of fire and the opposition of many authorities finally led to its abolition — although the bonfire custom led to the carrying of torches in the synagogue on Simḥat Torah. When this too was abolished on account of the danger; it was reduced to carrying candles inserted into fruit set atop a flag.

Hakhel — The Commandment to Assemble

In ancient times, Sukkot was the occasion for the observance of a biblical commandment that was to be performed only once in seven years. It is known as *hakhel* which means "gather" or "assemble" and refers to the commandment that all of Israel be assembled to listen to a public reading of the Torah. This as-

A Sukkot service at the North London Synagogue. Note the fact that only the cantor and the synagogue wardens have *lulavim*.

sembly was convened on the second day of Sukkot at the end of every Sabbatical year, when the land had to lie fallow.

> Every seventh year, the year set for remission, at the Feast of Booths, when all Israel comes to appear before the Lord your God in the place which He will choose, you shall read this Teaching aloud in the presence of all Israel. Gather the people — men, women, children, and the strangers in your communities, that they may hear and so learn to revere the Lord your God and to observe faithfully every word of this Teaching. . . .

This was the most propitious time for the assembly because even those who could not manage to make the pilgrimage on

The Great Assembly

Passover and Shavuot made an extra effort to do so on Sukkot, and the Sabbatical year probably enjoyed the largest pilgrimage.

The mass assembly was convened with the blowing of trumpets by the priests throughout Jerusalem. The reading of selected passages from the Book of Deuteronomy was done by the king. A large wooden platform would be set up in the Women's Courtyard of the Temple on which the king would sit with all the people gathered around. II Kings (chapter 23) describes one such event in which King Josiah participated.

The purpose of this assembly was to remind the people of the contents of the Torah and of their duties and obligations, and to reinspire them with its message. *The Purpose*

This commandment provides a striking example of the importance attached to mass knowledge and understanding of the Torah. Unlike some religious groups, knowledge of the basic documents of the Jewish faith was not to remain the preserve of a select few. All of the people were to be informed of their contents — for only in such knowledge was it possible to faithfully implement them. Even the women and the children were to be assembled to listen and to learn. None were excused from the obligation.

Maimonides regards the assembly as a reenactment of Israel's receiving the Torah at Sinai when all of the nation gathered to hear the Ten Commandments proclaimed. Therefore even scholars and sages well-versed in Torah were also under obligation to assemble and to listen intently to its reading.

The spirit of this regulation was extended by the men of the Great Assembly, under the leadership of Ezra, when they instituted the public reading of the Torah on each and every Sabbath, and on Mondays and Thursdays when people came into town for the market. Insofar as it serves both an educational as well as an inspirational purpose, the reason for the public reading of the Torah to this very day is no different than the observance of *hakhel*. *Basis of Torah Reading*

39

When Sukkot is not a Holiday

The word Sukkoth, also spelled Succoth, is the name of two places mentioned in the Bible. One is a locality in the Jordan Valley area of Israel; another is a place in Egypt between Ramses and Etham, the second stop of the Israelites on the route of the Exodus.

The word *Sukkah* is also the name of one of the tractates of the Talmud. It is the sixth tractate of the order of *Mo'ed,* and deals with the laws relating to the festival of Sukkot. Throughout the tractate the holiday is called simply *ḥag,* the Festival.

4.   THE SUKKAH

"You shall live in booths seven days . . ." is the most distinctive ritual observance of the festival. One is to eat and drink there, sleep there, and spend his leisure time there. "Throughout the seven days of the festival, the *sukkah* must be regarded as one's principal abode, and the house merely a temporary residence."

Rules of Living in Sukkah

Jewish law excuses one from living in the *sukkah* in case of illness *Dispensations* and provides a dispensation in case of rain or severe discomfort. A traveler on the road is likewise excused from eating in a *sukkah*

Copperplate engraving to the tractate *Sukkah* showing the preparation of the *sukkah,* from a title page of an 18th-century Hebrew-Latin edition of the Mishnah.

40

"Descendant of the High Priest" by Isidor Kaufmann, c. 1903. The young ḥasidic boy is holding the "four species" used on Sukkot.

Permanent collapsible *sukkah,* Fischach,
South Germany, c. 1800. The wall
painting depicts Jerusalem, the Temple
and the Western Wall. From a central
beam hangs a lamp of the "Judenstern"
type. This *sukkah* is exhibited at the
Israel Museum, Jerusalem.

This Tel Aviv *sukkah* is typical for Israel. Note the use of narrow wooden slats for *sekhakh*. One of the decorations hanging across the *sukkah* consists of emblems of Israel army regiments.

if none is available, as is a person who is only having some light refreshments that does not include bread. While the very pious in warmer climates make every effort to sleep in the *sukkah* too, the widespread practice has generally been limited to eating all of one's meals there, and to studying and socializing there.

This religious duty, like all positive *mitzvot* whose observance is based on a specific time period is not incumbent upon women. Nor is it obligatory on minor children. Nevertheless, except in such instances where the smallness of the *sukkah* or other personal hardships make it necessary for them to take advantage of the dispensation, the common practice is for the wife and the children to observe with equal fervor the duty of "dwelling in the *sukkah*" and for the entire family to enjoy together this annual observance.

Women and Children

As with all religious duties, a blessing is recited when this ritual is fulfilled. The special blessing is recited immediately fol-

41

The Four Species. Note the *pitom* (protuberance) on top of the *etrog* (which must be kept intact for the duration of the festival).

lowing the blessing over bread or over any other food or drink that is taken. The blessing is: "Blessed art Thou, O Lord our God, King of the Universe, Who has sanctified us with His commandments and commanded us to live in the *sukkah*."

There is an interesting and meaningful custom that takes the *The Special Guests* form of inviting into the *sukkah* each day one of the following biblical figures: Abraham, Isaac, Jacob, Moses, Aaron, Joseph and David. The custom is calledd *ushpizin*, which is the Aramaic word for "guests." It apparently originated with Isaac Luria and the kabbalists in the 16th century but is based on the *Zohar*.

> When a man sits in the shadow of faith, (a euphemism for *sukkah*), the *Shekhinah* (Divine Presence) spreads her wings on him from above and Abraham and five other righteous ones [and David with them] make their abode with him. . . . A man should rejoice each day of the festival with these guests who abide with him.

And so each evening, as one enters the *sukkah*, an invitation is extended to the souls of the above-mentioned ancestors to come and spend the evening in the booth. "Enter, enter, exalted holy guests. Come guests, high and holy. Come our fathers, high and holy. Come Abraham — and with him Isaac, Jacob, Moses, Aaron, Joseph and David. Please be seated, guests from on high. Be seated, be seated, holy guests. . . ." The invitations are extended according to the above-mentioned order, as suggested by the *Zohar* and still followed in the Sephardi liturgy. The Patriarchs are followed by Moses and Aaron, who in turn are followed by the two men who symbolize royalty — Joseph and David. The Ashkenazi liturgy however follows a chronological order so that Joseph is placed between Jacob and Moses, thus: Abraham, Isaac, Jacob, Joseph, Moses, Aaron, and David.

The inspiration for this custom is the example of hospitality *Hospitality* that was set by Abraham, the founder of the Jewish people, who would stand at the crossroads and invite guests to his table. The custom of *ushpizin* strengthens the people's identification with these ancestors and adds to their sense of being part of a great family that included royalty and spiritual giants. It also always encourages hospitality to the poor. The latter were often invited, as the *Zohar* continues, to teach that "the portion of those guests whom he invites must go to the poor."

The word *ushpizin* also came to be applied to those *sukkah* decorations or plaques that contain either the names of these seven men or the formal wording of the invitations.

Rules of Construction

The special "temporary" quality of the *sukkah* lies not in the walls, but in the roof or the ceiling which is called *sekhakh*. The sages pointed to the relationship between *sukkah*, the word used for tabernacle or booth, and *sekhakh*, the word used for the roof covering.

The material used for the roof covering must possess the *The Sekhakh* following characteristics: 1) it must *grow* from the earth (as opposed to being mined); 2) it must be *cut down* and no longer be connected to the ground; and 3) it must not be subject to ritual impurity. Anything lacking one of these three conditions cannot be used for *sekhakh*. Examples of such disqualified items would be: fruits and food (which is subject to ritual impurity); animal skins; metal; cloth; attached tree branches. Qualifying as suitable material to use as *sekhakh* would be branches cut from trees or bushes, straw, cornstalks, bamboo reeds, or narrow wood beams. Although poles and sticks can be used as *sekhakh*, more decorative types of *sekhakh* such as tree branches or boughs of evergreen leaves are mostly used.

Sekhakh is always put on after the walls are completed and *Thickness* never before, so that in putting on the *sekhakh*, the *sukkah* is completed. There should be sufficient *sekhakh* to provide more shade than sunlight inside the *sukkah*. An opening in the roof

44

which exceeds three *tefahim* (approximately 11 inches) disqualifies the *sukkah*. While some air space in the *sekhakh* is desirable so that the stars may be seen through it on a clear night, the *sukkah* is not disqualified if the *sekhakh* is too thick for that purpose. On the other hand, the *sekhakh* must not be so thick that it prevents rain from dripping in. This would also invalidate the *sukkah*.

A *sukkah* built indoors or under the overhang of a porch or balcony or under a tree is also not valid. The shade inside the *sukkah* must result from the kosher *sekhakh* and not from any material that does not qualify as *sekhahk*.

There are no restrictions on the material used for the walls of *The Walls* a *sukkah*. Any material such as metal, wood, canvas, brick or stone can be used. It must have at least two complete walls, with a third wall whose minimum width is one *tefah* (3 5/8 inches). The fourth side may be left open completely. Common practice however is to build four walls, with an opening or a doorway for the entrance. When a *sukkah* is constructed adjacent to a permanent house, one or more walls of the house may be considered as the walls of the *sukkah*.

Choosing *hoshanot*
(willows) from a street
salesman in New York.

In many European communities it was customary to build one small room of the house with a removable roof that could be manually or mechanically lifted or removed. *Sekhakh* would then be placed into the opening. In homes built around an atrium, it becomes similarly unnecessary to build any walls at all, as long as provision is made for covering the area with *sekhakh*. Most *sukkot* built today are, however, collapsible, made up of parts which can be easily assembled and taken apart.

The minimum area that can be used for a *sukkah* is seven *tefahim* (25 3/4 inches) by seven *tefahim*. This area is deemed sufficient to accommodate "the head of a person, the major portion of his body and his table." An area smaller than this is disqualified. There is no maximum area, and *sukkot* have been built to accommodate hundreds of people. Israeli restaurants, resort hotels and religious kibbutzim build such large *sukkot*.

In terms of height, there are maximum as well as minimum standards. The lowest to which a *sukkah* can be built is ten *tefahim* (approximately 36 7/8 inches). If they are lower than that, the walls lose their significance. By halakhic standards, any *mehizah* (divider or wall or barrier) that is less than ten *tefahim* is not legally regarded as a divider.

The highest to which a *sukkah* can be built is 20 cubits (approximately 36 1/4 feet). Several reasons are given for this height restriction: 1) Because it is written: "So that your future generations may know that I made the Israelite people to live in *sukkot* . . ."; one must know and beware of the fact that he is sitting in a *sukkah*. Until 20 cubits height, a person is automatically aware of it. Beyond that height, a person "is not aware that he is sitting in a *sukkah* as he does not generally cast his eyes up that high," and therefore does not see the *sekhakh* which is the essence of the *sukkah*. 2) Under 20 cubits height, a person is still sitting in the shade of the *sekhakh*; beyond that height, one is no longer in the shade of the *sekhakh*, but in the shade of the walls. 3) There is the halakhic consideration that any building

A balcony *sukkah* in Tel Aviv (top left) and two Sukkot scenes from the old section of the Meah She'arim quarter in Jerusalem.

higher than 20 cubits loses its status as a temporary dwelling. Though it may possess permanent walls, the *sukkah* must also qualify as a temporary dwelling.

No blessing is said when building the *sukkah* because the religious duty is performed by "living" in it and not by constructing it.

Decorating the Sukkah

The concept of *hiddur mitzvah* has traditionally played a role in Jewish ritual. This concept emphasizes the importance of achieving the greatest aesthetic perfection in the ritual object, thus "adorning" the *mitzvah*. The refinement and beauty in the ob- *Emphasis on the Aesthetic*

servance of all *mitzvot* is emphasized. In this spirit, it was regarded as praiseworthy to make the *sukkah* cheerful and inviting, a pleasant place in which to pass the hours. The interior walls of the *sukkah* are thus often decorated with pictures, tapestries, or flowers. Fruits and other decorations are also hung from the *sekhakh* above, or from the walls. Fruits and sweets used for such decoration may not be eaten during the entire week of Sukkot. The festive table and the lights add the final touches to the festive atmosphere.

Decoration of the *sukkah* is a practice that has its source in *Fruit and* the Talmud, which indicates that nuts and pomegranates and *Tapestries* grape clusters used to be hung from the *sekhakh*. Oriental communities introduced the use of colorful wall tapestries. In European communities, artistic decorations and pictures prevailed. The Israel Museum in Jerusalem exhibits a particularly artistic *sukkah*. It originated from Fishbach in Southern Germany and dates from the early 19th century. The structure is collapsible, complete with numbered boards and beams, and its walls are elaborately decorated with paintings depicting the city of Jerusalem, the Temple, the Western Wall, the Levites, Moses on Mount Sinai, Elijah in the valley of Kerith, and a secular scene of a man going hunting while his wife waits for him outside their house.

It was regarded as particularly meritorious and praiseworthy *At the* to start on the construction of the *sukkah* immediately after *Conclusion of* Yom Kippur — thereby engaging in a religious duty upon the *Yom Kippur* conclusion of the fast day. But no matter when it is done, *sukkah* building and decorating is a project of religious significance in which the whole family can participate. It is generally an eagerly awaited occasion for the children and provides them with memorable experiences.

Families living in suburban areas or in single homes that pos- *Modern* sess a patio or garden area or open porch are ideally situated for *Problems* building their own *sukkah*. Jews living in apartment houses in

"The Meal in the Sukkah"; a drawing by Bernard Picart showing the contrast between an opulent rich man's *sukkah* (note the maid) and a poor man's *sukkah* in the background.

dense urban areas are confronted with a problem. They have been known to erect *sukkot* on the roofs of their buildings or their backyards, very often to the annoyance of landlords. Proverbial stories about lawsuits to remove them and the decisions of judges ordering such removal in ten days are legion. Particularly for the benefit of those families who have no place to erect their own *sukkot*, it became customary for a *sukkah* to be built at the synagogue, thus enabling the congregants to bring their meals there, or at least to partake there of the *Kiddush* following the services.

In the cities of modern-day Israel, it is customary for some *Competitions* city administrations to run *sukkah* contests, awarding prizes to those most beautifully decorated. In Israel today, one sees *sukkot* constructed on sidewalks, roofs, courtyards, and balconies reminiscent of the scene described in Nehemiah: "So the people went forth . . . and made themselves booths, every one upon the roof of his house, and in their courts, and in the courts of the house of God."

5. THE FOUR SPECIES

The Four Species is the second most distinctive ritual observance of Sukkot. The Torah directs that on the first day of the festival, Jews are to take four different species in hand and with them to rejoice before the Lord: "On the first day, you shall take the product of *hadar* trees, branches of palm trees, and boughs of leafy trees, and willows of the brook, and you shall rejoice before the Lord your God seven days."

The word *hadar* means beautiful, and the biblical passage *Hadar* could therefore mean the fruit of any goodly tree. Tradition however identified the fruit as the citron, called in Hebrew *etrog*. The boughs of leafy trees were identified with myrtle twigs, called in Hebrew, *hadassim*. The palm branch is called a *lulav*; the

50

"The Jew with the Palm"; a lithograph by Alphons Levi. Note the Sabbath lamp suspended over the table and the *Mizrah* plaque on the wall indicating the direction for prayer.

A selection of *etrog* boxes. 1. Silver-plated, Galicia, 19th century;
2. Silver, Central Europe, 19th century;
3. Silver, Meknes, Morocco, 19th/20th century; 4. Silver repousse, Turkey, 19th century; 5. Gilded glass set in silver, Germany, c.1830; 6. Silver, Austria, 19th century.

willows are called *aravot*. Together, these are called *arba'ah minim*, the "Four Species" (of plant).

Symbolism of the Four Species

The Four Species were undoubtedly intended to symbolize the *A Bond with* final harvest, the fertility of the land in a ritual of thanksgiving. *the Earth* Maimonides sees the four species as "the basis of the holiday joy for fruits and flowers lift man's spirit and instill joy in the heart of man." That these four were chosen for that purpose may have been due to their staying power, i.e., they are able to retain their moisture and freshness for the seven days, and because they were easily found in the Land of Israel.

A common Israeli street scene in the week before Sukkot. Note the exceptionally large *etrogim*, sometimes weighing as much as 5 lbs., a type favored by Yemenite Jews.

54

Even in an urban environment where people are removed from direct contact with the soil, flowers and fruits are still a symbol of joy. They still serve "to lift man's spirit and instil joy in his heart." The use of flowers at all festive occasions, as an expression of love to a beloved, as a gift to cheer the sick, as a symbol of peace and tranquility, of simple human pleasures, serves to emphasize the validity of Maimonides' insight. The agricultural symbolism of the Four Species — even to the city dweller, perhaps especially to him — provides a momentary connection with the soil and the delight that it offers. To hold these particular plants in hand is to also identify with the Land of Israel.

The Midrash explains the significance of the Four Species *Four Types of* with a number of homiletic interpretations that convey moral *People* lessons. The most popular interpretation is the one based on the qualities of the four plants. The *etrog* possesses both taste and good odor; the palm (i.e., the date) only taste; the myrtle only odor; and the willow possesses neither quality. Taste and odor respectively symbolize Torah and good works. The Four Species are thus said to represent the different categories of Jews insofar as they possess both, one or the other, or none of these two virtues. Yet as the Four Species are treated as one whole unit, so are the Jewish people regarded as a unit who are bidden to come together to worship and rejoice before the Lord. The failings of one are compensated for by the virtues of the others. All are needed to be brought together if a blessing over the whole unit is to be made. No blessing can be said if even one of the categories is separated from the others. Thus, a lesson in Jewish unity, despite disparate elements, is taught.

Still another interpretation is based on the different shapes of *The Four Limbs* each of the four species. The *lulav* resembles the spine; the *etrog* has the shape of the heart; the myrtle leaves are shaped like the eye; and the willow corresponds to the mouth. All of these organs should be brought to bear in the service of the Lord: the

55

sincerity of the heart; the words of the mouth; the inspiration of the scene viewed by the eyes; the erect posture or required bowings made possible by the spine.

The Ritual

Three myrtle twigs and two willows are tied to the *lulav* with the myrtle set slightly higher than the willow. It is now customary to set them into a holder made from a palm leaf that is slipped on to the *lulav*. In Temple times, wealthy Jews used golden chains to tie them together. Among Yemenite Jews, the myrtle and willow twigs are tied around the *lulav* in the form of a bouquet. While no more than two willow twigs may be taken, Maimonides rules that the myrtle twigs used may be increased to any number.

Holding this unit in the right hand, side by side with the *etrog* in the left hand, the following blessing is recited every day of Sukkot (except for the Sabbath): "Blessed art Thou, O Lord our God, King of the Universe, Who has sanctified us with His commandments and commanded us concerning the taking of the *lulav*." *The Benediction*

The wording of the blessing refers only to the *lulav*. Since it is the largest of the four, the entire group is called by its name. On the first day of the festival only, the benediction of *she-heḥeyanu* (see page 88) is added.

The proper way to hold the *lulav* is with the spine facing the holder. The proper way to hold the *etrog* is with the *pitom* (the nipple which sticks out at one end) on top, and the stem or the stalk where it had been attached to the tree, on the bottom.

Since the moment one takes hold of the *etrog* and *lulav* together, one has in effect fulfilled his religious duty, a question of procedure arose because the blessing is supposed to be said before the ritual is performed. To solve the dilemma, different procedures were suggested: 1) to first take only the *lulav*, recite the blessing, and only then pick up the *etrog*; 2) mentally intend not to fulfill this *mitzvah* until after the blessing is recited; 3) be- *Solutions to a Dilemma*

56

Embroidered hanging for a *sukkah,*
silk, gold, and silver thread on
taffeta, 18th century, Italy. It
depicts the *Simhat Beit ha-Sho'evah,*
the Feast of the Drawing of Water,
and shows three men performing
dances and acrobatics as described
by Rabbi Simeon ben Gamaliel,
head of the Sanhedrin.

"Rejoicing of the Law in the Ancient Synagogue of Leghorn"
(Italy); oil painting by Solomon Alexander Hart (1806-1881).

fore the blessing, hold the *etrog* upside down with the stem on top so that it is being held improperly, and only after the blessing, turn it over so that it is held properly. Accepted procedure follows this last opinion.

While the religious obligation is basically fulfilled by reciting the blessing and properly taking hold of the Four Species, the sages also called for waving it three times to and fro in all directions, and upwards and downwards. These wavings are of very ancient tradition and will be discussed further in the chapter.

According to tradition, the biblical requirement to "rejoice before the Lord your God seven days," with the Four Species in hand, applied only to the Temple where this was done every day.

In Temple Times

For the people outside the Temple, the requirement was limited to the first day only. After the destruction of the Temple, Rabbi Johanan ben Zakkai ordained that no matter where Sukkot is celebrated, the Four Species should be taken in hand for all the seven days in commemoration of the Temple. This is the practice to this day.

The religious authorities of the Middle Ages disagreed on the question whether the city of Jerusalem beyond the Temple Mount was in the same category as the Temple, or in the category of *medinah*, outside of the Temple. Maimonides ruled that in connection with the Four Species Jerusalem possessed the same status as the Temple. Rashi regarded Jerusalem's status as distinct from that of the Temple. According to the view of Maimonides, Jerusalemites to this day have a biblical duty to take the *lulav-etrog* all seven days, and only for those living beyond Jerusalem is the biblical requirement limited to the first day, with the requirement for the last six days being of rabbinic origin. *Jerusalem and the Temple Mount*

The Four Species were not taken up on that day of Sukkot which fell on the Sabbath, except in the Temple area itself. This *The Sabbath*

A hammered and embossed silver *etrog* container from Holland, 1889. In the center are the initials of the owner.

stems from the talmudic edict which sought to prevent the desecration of the Sabbath. If it would be taken, its use might require it to be carried into the public domain to and from the synagogue thus violating the Sabbath prohibition against carrying. The same reason applied to the elimination of the *shofar* blowing on Rosh Ha-Shanah when it coincided with the Sabbath. These edicts did not take into consideration the widespread use of a Sabbath *eruv*, which is the technical enclosure of an entire city or major portions thereof, enabling it to be classified under religious law as a "private" area.

The *lulav* and *etrog* are also taken up and held in the hand during that portion of the worship service known as *Hallel* (Psalms 113–118), the psalms in praise of God said every day of the festival during the morning service, immediately following the *Amidah*.

At several points during the *Hallel*, the *lulav* and *etrog* are *The Wavings* pointed three times in all directions accompanied by a slight shaking or waving of the *lulav*. This procedure is known as the *na'anuim* (literally: the wavings), and is done while reciting the verse: "Give thanks unto the Lord for He is good, for His kindness endures forever," (the beginning of Psalm 118), and verse 25 of that same psalm: "We beseech Thee, O Lord, save us. . . ."

The waving of the Four Species is done in a prescribed man- *In All* ner: three times to and fro towards the east, then three times to *Directions* and fro each towards the south, the west, the north, upwards and downwards.

In a synagogue where the Ark is on the east wall, as is usually the case, the direction of the wavings can be simply described as follows: ahead, then clockwise to right side, back, the left side, then upwards, and downwards. Sephardi ritual varies slightly. There the *na'anuim* always follows the order: right, left, ahead, back, upwards, downwards.

In present-day prayer services, these *na'anuim* are performed every day of the festival (except for the Sabbath) during the recitation of the *Hallel.* It is also customary to perform them immediately after reciting the daily blessings over the *lulav.* These wavings in all directions are said to symbolize the presence of God in all directions and as a way of rejoicing with the Four Species before God as the Torah commands. They may possibly also represent the "clouds of glory" which the Midrash says descended on Sukkot from all four directions, and above and below. Others saw the waving as an allusion to the verse in I Chronicles: "Then shall the trees of the forest sing for joy, before the Lord, for He is come to judge the earth," which is immediately followed by the same verse that appears in Psalms and during which the wavings are performed: "O give thanks unto the Lord; for He is good; for His mercy endureth forever." Still others have seen it as a custom that formed part of the ancient ritual prayers for rain. One talmudic source interpreted the wavings as a rite by which "evil winds" were warded off.

In the Temple, the Four Species were taken up again after *The Procession* the *Musaf* offering. This time it was for a procession around the altar while Psalm 118:25, *Ana Adonai hoshi'ah na,* "Please God save us," or the words *Ani va-hu hoshi'ah na,* a popular version of the same verse, were chanted. One circuit of the altar was made on each of the first six days; seven circuits on the seventh day.

This ancient Temple ritual is reenacted in synagogues today, when immediately following the *Amidah* of the *Musaf* service, the Ark is opened, a Torah scroll is taken out and held on the *bimah* which represents the altar, while worshipers holding *lulavim* and *etrogim* form a procession around the *bimah*. Different passages praying for rain, for a good harvest, for divine deliverance, are chanted both before and during the procession. This section of the service is known as *Hoshanot*, from the refrain in the prayer *hoshana* or *hoshi'ah na* which means "O save us." Although the procession is omitted on the Sabbath, a special Hoshana prayer for the Sabbath is generally recited.

Sephardi ritual developed the custom of reciting the *Hoshanot* during the *Shaḥarit* service, immediately after the *Hallel*. The apparent reason for this shift was the convenience of combining the two parts of the service that required taking the *lulav* and *etrog* in hand.

The Etrog

Of all the Four Species, the *etrog* merited special attention on the part of the masses. Because of the biblical use of the word *hadar*, beautiful, to describe the tree, Jews throughout the centuries paid extra attention to the aesthetic qualities of the *etrog* and took extra care to select an *etrog* that was as close to perfect as possible. The emphasis on *hiddur mitzvah* (see page 48) in connection with the fruit of the *hadar* tree was widespread. To this day, pious men make a special point of shopping for and selecting their own *etrog*. The markets in the religious quarters of Jerusalem and Tel Aviv, as the stores that sell religious items in the Diaspora, are a beehive of activity on the days preceding Sukkot. Mingling around the stalls selling *etrogim* are multitudes of rabbis and scholars, religious men young and old, carefully selecting and examining *etrogim* much as a diamond merchant carefully inspects a prospective purchase. Nor is the analogy farfetched. To the faithful, the *etrog* is as precious as a diamond.

Selecting the Etrog

61

The experts examine an *etrog*.

The beauty of the *etrog* is judged not by its size, but how evenly shaped it is, by whether or not it has any blemishes or spots, and by the convolutions of the skin. Just as there are men who are regarded as art experts, so are some deferred to as greater *etrog* experts whose opinion as to the *etrog's* quality and worth are sought. Apart from all other considerations, the cost of an *etrog* to this day varies according to its aesthetic qualities. It may be very large, requiring both hands to hold it, or as small as an egg.

There are some flaws, of course, that render the *etrog* totally unfit for ritual use. Examples of such flaws are: a hole, or per- foration that runs through the *etrog*, if any part of it is missing, or if the larger part of it is covered with scars, if it is dried up, peeled or split, or if it is round like a ball. But the easiest damage that an *etrog* can suffer to render it ritually unfit is to have its *pitom* broken off. That is why such great care is taken with it after it is bought. It is carefully wrapped in flax and gingerly placed in a box or container specially reserved for the *etrog*.

The *etrog* container, in fact, has become one of the ritual objects to which artists devoted considerable talent. The variety ranges from rectangular boxes to containers shaped like the *etrog* itself, made either from metal or wood, each decorated differ- ently. The rich use *etrog* containers made from silver.

One may not borrow someone else's *lulav* and *etrog* with which to fulfill the ritual obligation on the first day of the festi- val, but may receive it as a gift. In "borrowing" it from another, it is therefore necessary for the owner to stipulate that it is being offered as a gift and not as a loan. When a synagogue purchases one for the use of its worshipers, since it is bought with public funds, each congregant is considered a part owner.

When the *etrog* is cut from the tree, its color is green. As it ripens over a period of time, it turns a bright yellow and it is at this stage that it is ideal for use on Sukkot. After Sukkot, many women collect discarded *etrogim* in order to make a most de-

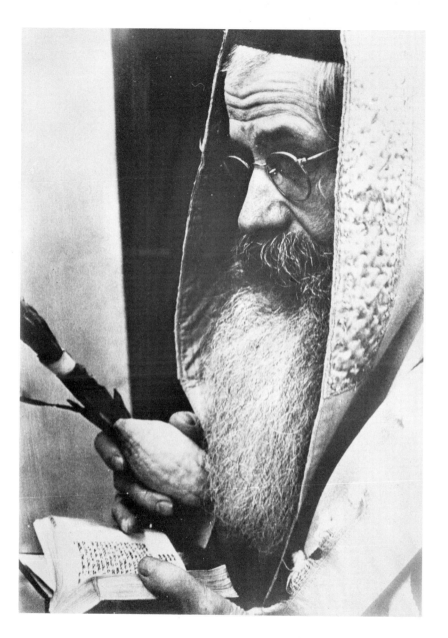

Holding the Four Species during the prayers. A
congregant at the Lubavitch synagogue in New York.

Israel's Sukkot markets.
Careful shoppers examine the
Four Species closely to ensure
that they are ritually fit. There
are also special markets for
sekhakh.

65

licious jam from them. That the *etrog* used to be eaten after the holiday is indicated by the Talmud. If it is not eaten and allowed to stay, it slowly dries up and withers, turning dark brown in color and becoming very small and rock hard.

Although the *etrog* is plentiful today, being grown in great *In the Middle Ages* abundance not only in Israel, but also in such semi-tropical areas as Southern California, Florida, Greece and Italy, there were many periods in Jewish history when it was extremely difficult to obtain one. This was particularly true of European Jewish communities during the Middle Ages and almost into modern times. Men would go to great expense and great trouble to get the rare fruit shipped to them. It was not at all unusual to find entire Jewish communities with just one *etrog* in its midst. The personal sacrifice that often went into the acquisition of an *etrog* and the loving care it was shown after being acquired became almost legendary, immortalized in many a short story by Jewish writers.

Religious controversy relating to the *etrog* centered on two *The Grafted Etrog* questions. One had to do with the acceptability of the species of *etrog* that grows without a *pitom*. Although an *etrog* whose *pitom* has broken off is rendered unfit for ritual use, an *etrog* that naturally grows that way is regarded as acceptable. The second issue arose at the beginning of the 19th century when the grafting of lemon branches onto citron trees began to be practiced. Such an *etrog* is called *murkav* — grafted. Non-Jewish grove owners in the Mediterranean area began the practice to improve the appearance of the citron. A grafted *etrog* can be recognized by the following characteristics: its skin is smooth with no bulges or protusions; its stem is not imbedded into the fruit; its skin is thin; the flesh is very juicy..

Most religious authorities found the practice objectionable and ruled that such *etrogim* were ritually invalid. A major controversy erupted in 1809 over *etrogim* from the Greek island of Corfu, a rumor having spread in the Jewish world that *etrogim* from there came from allegedly grafted trees. The controversy over the reliability of Corfu *etrogim* divided religious authorities for many decades. Towards the latter part of the 19th century, in the 1870's, *etrogim* from the Land of Israel began to appear on the market. The Chief Rabbi of Jerusalem at the time, Rabbi Meir Averbach, and many other European religious authorities urged the purchase of these *etrogim* both on account of their not being under suspicion of having come from grafted trees, but also because they found religious spiritual grounds for preferring an *etrog* from the Holy Land to one that was grown elsewhere. *Holy Land Etrogim*

The support for Holy Land *etrogim* expressed by such authorities as Rabbi Isaac Elḥanan Spektor of Kovno, Rabbi Naphtali Ẓevi Berlin of Volozin, and Rabbi Ḥayyim Soloveichik of Brisk eventually helped establish the supremacy of Israeli *etrogim* and turned it into one of the first successful industries established by the returning Jewish settlers at the end of the 19th and beginning of the 20th centuries.

Flaws that Invalidate

The flaws that invalidate a *lulav* are the following: if it is dried up; if the palm leaves are not attached to the spine; if most of the outside leaves were cut off; if the top was cut off; if the top of the spine was bent; or if the spine was split down the middle. *The Lulav*

The flaws that invalidate *hadassim* are the following: if its leaves were dried up or cut off; if its berries are more numerous than its leaves. It is considered particularly desirable for the *hadas* to have three leaves of equal size coming out of the same socket along the stem, or if the leaves have their individual sockets, they should be close to one other around the stem so that none of the three leaves is either shorter or taller than the others. The leaves themselves should be wide at the center and narrow at the sides, similar to the shape of an eye. *The Hadassim*

The flaws that invalidate the *aravah* are the following: if its edges are jagged; if its top was cut off; or if most of its leaves *The Aravot* dried up or fell off. The *aravah* of the brook should be of that species that has a smooth-edged leaf.

6. HOSHANA RABBA

The Seventh Day of the Willow

The seventh day of Sukkot when seven circuits of the altar take place has become known as Hoshana Rabba, meaning the Great Hoshana, on account of the great number of *hoshanot* prayers recited on that day. In the Talmud, the day is called *yom ha-shevi'i shel aravah*, the seventh day of the willow. The special significance assigned to this day by the masses is noted in the Talmud where it is mentioned as one of the two days on which everyone attended the synagogue service. The first was the "day of blowing the *shofar*," and the second was "the day of the willow."

This association of Hoshana Rabba with Rosh Ha-Shanah is indicative of the early development of the belief that Hoshana Rabba was also a day of judgment (see page 20), relating to rain.

The ritual and prayers for rain that reflected this belief found *From Moses at* expression in two distinct ceremonies that took place in the *Sinai* Temple throughout the week of Sukkot and reach their climax on Hoshana Rabba. One was the ritual of the *aravot*, the other was the water-libation (pouring) ceremony (*nisukh ha-mayim*). Both these rituals were classified as "laws given to Moses at Sinai." This designation was given to a number of very ancient traditions that possessed biblical authority but were neither explicitly stated in Scripture, nor derived from Scripture by hermeneutical principles, nor were the result of rabbinic legislation.

Great emphasis was attached to these ceremonies. For they were not only thankful for and celebrating the ingathering of the past harvest, but they were also deeply concerned about a sufficient rainfall in the months ahead to assure adequate water for the next season's crop and to guarantee the replenishment of the water reserves in their cisterns which had almost run dry through the hot, rainless summer months.

The Ritual of the Willow

It was the practice in the Temple to take willows for ritual use all seven days of the festival apart from the willow that was used with the Four Species. As the willow grows near brooks and streams, its association with ceremonies for water is under- *The Ceremony* standable. The Talmud describes the ritual as follows: Willow branches were specially cut each day at Moẓa near Jerusalem and were fixed at the side of the altar so that their leaves hung over the top of the altar. It is indicated that these *aravot* were 11 cubits tall (246 1/2 inches) extending one cubit above the altar, which was ten cubits (224 inches) high. The *shofar* was blown and a single procession around the altar took place. During the procession the passage from Psalms: *Ana Adonai hoshi'ah na, Ana Adonai haẓliḥah na*, "Pray, O Lord, save us, Pray, O Lord, make us succeed" was chanted. On the seventh day of Sukkot, the procession would circle the altar seven times. At the conclusion, the participants would cry out: "Thine O Altar is the beauty! Thine O Altar is the beauty!" Except for the fact that the willows were gathered the day before, the ceremony of the willow took place even on the Sabbath day.

Rabbinic opinion differed as to whether the willows were *The Order* first carried around the altar and then set up at its sides or whether the act of setting up the *aravot* preceded the procession. Maimonides was of the latter opinion. According to him, the procession itself took place only with the *lulav* and *etrog*. Opinion also differed as to who participated in the altar processions. Some thought that only the priests did. Others maintained that "the elders of Jerusalem," even non-priests, circled the altar with their *lulavim*.

Rabbi Johanan ben Beroka said that in addition to the willow *Palm-twigs* rite, palm twigs were brought and beaten upon the ground at the

A copper engraved *sukkah* decoration. Germany or Holland, 18th century.

side of the altar and that the day was called *yom ḥavut ḥarayot,* "the day of the beating of the palm twigs." The latter custom is of inexplicable origin, probably an ancient water rite (see page 20). It is said to have been a custom of the Prophets.

After the destruction of the Temple, the obligation of the *aravah* ritual lapsed. But to commemorate the Temple practice, rabbinic authority established it for one day only, on the seventh day. This is the basis for the contemporary custom that after the final circuit with the *lulav* and *etrog* and the recitation of the *hoshanot* on the last day of Sukkot, the willow is taken in hand and special prayers that almost exclusively concern themselves with water are recited. It also provides the background for the custom of beating the *aravot* twice upon the ground, or accord-

70

ing to some, five times at the conclusion of that part of the service. It is now customary for the sexton of the synagogue to provide *aravot* for sale to the worshipers on Hoshana Rabba morning. The willows used on Hoshana Rabba are also called *hoshanot*. From this derives the expression "a beaten *hoshana*" to describe a person who has come down in the world.

The Water Libation Ceremony

Another main feature of the Temple service throughout the week of Sukkot was the *nisukh ha-mayim*, the water-libation ceremony. While the pouring of wine upon the altar was part of the daily sacrificial ritual, the use of water in the same fashion is nowhere mentioned in the Torah. Yet the tradition of water libation was apparently a very ancient one and is treated as among the oral laws given to Moses at Sinai. Water is one of God's greatest gifts and its pouring out on the altar symbolized a form of offering or sacrifice. Examples of such a water offering are found elsewhere in biblical literature. When Samuel was about to pray for Israel in Mizpeh, "they drew water and poured it out before the Lord, and fasted on that day. . . ." When David's three friends broke through the camp of the Philistines and brought him water from the well of Bethlehem, he did not drink it but "poured it out unto the Lord." Gideon, wishing to make a sacrifice to God, was told by the angel of God, "Take the flesh and the unleavened cakes and place them upon the rock, and pour out the broth." It is assumed that the pouring of the broth was a libation which God accepted as He did the flesh and cakes which were burned by the fire from the rock.

Even the four pitchers of water that Elijah poured over the sacrifice and the wood on Mount Carmel may also have constituted part of his offering to God, and not only the enhancement of the miracle of the divine fire.

The water for the Temple ritual was drawn from the pools of Shiloah, a natural well at the foot of Jerusalem. The vessel used to draw the water was a golden flask. The amount of water drawn and poured on the altar was three *lugin*, about three pints. All the while, the Levites played on their flutes and harps and trumpets and cymbals. They stood on the fifteen steps descending from the Israelites' Court to the Women's Court, symbolizing the fifteen Psalms which begin with the words *Shir ha-Ma'alot*, A Song of Ascents. At each part of the water libation ritual, priests blew the trumpets.

Rejoicing of the Place of the Water-Drawing

Perhaps the most memorable feature of the ceremonies was the rejoicing that accompanied them. The biblical inspiration for the festivities may well have been the verse from Isaiah, "With joy shall you draw water out of the wells of salvation. "The gala celebration was called the *Simhat Bet ha-Sho'eva*, the "Rejoicing of the Place of the Water-drawing." It gave full expression to the biblical directive that "you shall rejoice in your festival" and highlighted the holiday's title as "the season of our rejoicing." Its ecstasy was captured by the following brief passage in the Talmud: "One who has not seen the rejoicing of the *Bet ha-Sho'eva* has never seen a rejoicing in his life."

Huge golden candelabras with four golden cups on each were *The Rejoicing* set up in the Temple court and when they were lit, there was not a courtyard in Jerusalem that was not lit up by their light. Men of piety and good works would dance, holding burning torches in their hands and singing songs of praise to God. Wilder antics and feats of skill were also part of the scene. The Talmud relates that Rabbi Simeon ben Gamaliel, the dignified president of the Sanhedrin in the first century of the common era, would juggle eight burning torches at a time, "throwing them in the air and catching them as they came down."

Rabbi Joshua ben Hananiah said: "When we rejoiced at the *Simhat Bet ha-Sho'eva* we did not know sleep. In the first hour was the morning offering (and the water libation); then the

72

The Siloam (Shilo'ah) pool in Jerusalem from which water for Temple rituals was taken. A 19th century French engraving.

73

prayer; then the *Musaf* offering followed by the Musaf prayer; then to the House of Study and from there to eat and drink; thence to the afternoon offering and from then onwards (through the night) to the *Simḥat Bet ha-Sho'eva.*"

Since the *Simḥat Bet ha-Sho'eva* did not take precedence over the Sabbath or the *yom tov*, it took place only five or six nights, depending on whether the first day of the festival fell on a weekday or on a Sabbath. In our own day, pious Jews commemorate the *Simḥat Bet ha-Sho'eva* of the Temple period by gathering on one of the intermediate nights of Sukkot for a festive evening, marked by food and drink, by song and dance. In the ḥasidic quarters of Jerusalem one can hear the sound of bands playing loud and clear as crowded halls accommodate the

many hundreds who join in the singing and the dancing into all hours of the night. These festivities are also called *Simḥat Bet ha-Sho'eva.*

Hoshana Rabba Customs

The "judgment day" aspect with which Hoshana Rabba is associ- ated gave rise to a number of distinctive practices, some followed to this day.

As on Rosh Ha-Shanah, it is customary on this day to eat honey, symbolizing a sweet year. Psalm 27, which is recited daily beginning a month before Rosh Ha-Shanah in preparation for the period of repentance and judgment, is continued through Hoshana Rabba (through Shemini Aẓeret in the Diaspora).

The white mantles on the Torah scrolls, and the white *parokhet* on the Ark that was put on for the High Holy Day period remain on till after Hoshana Rabba and Shemini Aẓeret.

In taking out the scrolls of the Torah from the Ark, the High Holy Day passages are said. As on the Day of Atonement, numerous candles are kindled in the synagogue. In some rites, the *ḥazzan* wears a white robe, a melody used on the Day of Atonement is chanted, the verses said on the Ten Days of Penitence: "Remember us unto life . . ." etc. are inserted and the *shofar* is blown during the processions. In some places, it was customary to conclude the service with the same passages with which the Day of Atonement is concluded.

It is the custom among the pious to stay awake throughout Hoshana Rabba night, spending it in prayer and study, particularly in reading through the Book of Deuteronomy.

A rather strange legend became widespread during the Middle Ages, sometime after the 13th century, to the effect that if one did not see the shadow of his head on the night of Hoshana Rabba, he would not live out the year.

All in all, rabbinic authorities throughout the ages vested the day with such significance that they so arranged the Hebrew

Young Ḥasidim dance with joy and abandon at a Simḥat Bet Ha-Sho'eva celebration held during *ḥol ha-mo'ed.* The popular "bottle dance" is perhaps evocative of the water libations.

calendar to prevent Hoshana Rabba from ever falling out on a Sabbath for this would necessitate the suspension of the special rituals associated with it.

7. LITURGICAL ASPECTS OF SUKKOT

Kohelet

The custom of reading one of the Five Scrolls (*Megillot*) on the different festivals extends back to the talmudic era. Thus, the Song of Songs is read on Passover; Ruth is read on Shavuot; Lamentations on Tish'ah be-Av; Esther on Purim; and Ecclesiastes or Kohelet, was selected for Sukkot.

It is read on the intermediate Sabbath of the festival. Where

The opening page of *Ecclesiastes Rabba,* a midrash to Ecclesiastes. This is the first published edition; Pesaro, 1519.

76

the first day of Sukkot falls on a Sabbath so that there is no intermediate Sabbath, its reading takes place in Israel on the first day, and in the Diaspora on Shemini Azeret.

Kohelet is both the name of the book and of the author who *Solomon* describes himself as the son of David, king in Jerusalem. Tradition identifies Kohelet with King Solomon who wrote it towards the end of his life.

The book was the subject of great rabbinic controversy be- *Acceptance* fore it was accepted into the canon of the Bible. It is a philo- *into the Canon* sophical search for meaning in life, an evaluation of the different options open to man; a discussion of the wide range of Kohelet's experiments and experiences with both wisdom and folly. Many of its hypotheses are heretical; at the very least suggestive of doubt, rather than abiding faith. It projects both piety and skepticism; both the joy of life and the bitterness of despair and disappointment. It realistically reflects the alternating moods of man which shift so very often between the materialistic and the spiritual, between the desire to pamper one's flesh by pursuing the path of pleasure and self-indulgence, or to respond to the moral and nobler urges. Hedonism and fatalism are set up against spiritual duty and reverence for God.

Some of its passages have become famous among many peoples, popular aphorisms known even to those who are otherwise unfamiliar with the Bible. To quote just a few:

"Vanity of vanities, all is vanity."
"There is nothing new under the sun."
"To everything there is a season . . . A time to be born, and a
    time to die . . ."
"As he came forth . . . naked shall he go back as he came, and
    shall take nothing for his labor . . ."
"A good name is better than precious oil."

The decisive factor that won for this book admission into the Canon as one of the books of the Sacred Scriptures is the conclusion drawn by Kohelet from all his musings, from all his doubts and misgivings: "The end of the matter, all having been heard: fear God, and keep His commandments; for this is the whole man."

As a book filled with pessimism and despair, Kohelet may at first glance seem to be an inappropriate choice for the festival of rejoicing. The selection was perhaps due to the fact that the sages wanted to strike a balance in a period of gaiety and celebration

Plaque from a Hamburg synagogue to remind the congregation to insert the prayer for rain into the *Amidah*. Carved walnut, 18th century.

when it is easy to immerse oneself in physical pleasures and lose sight of life's ultimate values. The Book of Kohelet serves to keep in focus both the form and the purpose of the celebration.

The Additional Sukkot Liturgy

The contents of the *hoshanot* prayers include prayers of a general nature, and also supplications for water, for a good harvest, for salvation from exile, and for redemption. *Hoshanot* on various subjects and in different forms have been composed. Those recited today are credited to Eleazar Ha-Kallir. For the Sabbath day, a special *hoshana* prayer that refers to the Sabbath is recited, although in some liturgical rites, *hoshanot* are not recited on the Sabbath of Sukkot at all (see pages 60, 68).

Hallel means praise and refers to a collection of Psalms *Hallel* (chapters 113-118) that is preceded by and concluded with a blessing. It is said immediately following the *Amidah* of *Shaharit*, on each of the days of Sukkot and on Shemini Azeret—Simhat Torah. Except for the Sabbath day, the *lulav* and *etrog* are taken up and held during its recitation throughout Sukkot.

An additional passage inserted into the blessing of *rezei*, the *Ya'aleh ve-Yavo* third from the last blessing in the Morning, Afternoon and Evening *Amidah*, which asks God to receive in love Israel's prayers and its offerings and to restore the divine service at Jerusalem. It is not inserted in the *Musaf* service. The passage is called *Ya'aleh ve-yavo*, "ascend and come," because these are the first words that follow "Our God and God of our Fathers" at the very beginning of the passage.

This passage is also inserted in the third blessing of the Grace after Meals which also speaks of the restoration of Zion and Jerusalem so that it parallels the *Amidah* blessing.

During the repetition of the *Amidah*, when the reader comes to the phrases in the *Ya'aleh ve-yavo* that read: "Remember us, O Lord our God, for our good, be mindful of us for blessing, and save us unto life" — the congregation, at the conclusion of each phrase, responds with "Amen."

Scriptural Readings for Sukkot

The Torah reading for the first day of the holiday is from Leviticus 22:26 through 23:44. The same portion is read in the Diaspora on the second day. Five people are called up for *aliyot*. If the festival falls on a Sabbath day, seven people are called to the Torah. Following the first few verses that contain prohibitions relating to the slaughtering of an animal and its offspring

79

on the same day, and to the desecration of God's Name, the reading is devoted to a review of all the sacred days and festivals that God commands Israel to observe. In the order mentioned, they are: the Sabbath, Passover, Shavuot, the Day of Blowing the *Shofar* (Rosh Ha-Shanah), the Day of Atonement, and Sukkot— Shemini Azeret.

From a second scroll, the passage from Numbers 29:12-16 is read. This describes the offerings which were to be brought to the Temple on this day. On the intermediate days of the festival, the verses appropriate for the day are read from the rest of the same chapter.

The *Geshem* prayer recited on Shemini Azeret. Note the signs of the zodiac. Sukkot *mahzor* with Yiddish translation, Vilna 1907.

Frontispiece of a Sukkot *maḥzor* printed in Sulzbach, Germany, 1826. The engraving by Joseph Herz (1776–1828) shows *hakkafot*.

The *Haftarah* (selection from the Prophets) read on the first day is from Zechariah 14. This describes the messianic vision of the Prophet that the nations will join together to make war on Jerusalem. After an initial defeat, Jerusalem will emerge victorious. Following that there will be a recognition that "God is King over all the earth . . . that He is one and His Name one." The nations of the earth will then assemble in Jerusalem to celebrate Sukkot.

On the second day in the Diaspora, the *Haftarah* is from I Kings 8:2-21. This selection describes the dedication of the First Temple by Solomon, which took place on Sukkot.

81

On the intermediate Sabbath of the festival, two scrolls are
also used. From the first, the reading is from Exodus 33:12
through 34:26. It describes the directives of Moses to carve out
the second set of Ten Commandments, and refers to the "thirteen attributes of God." The chapter was selected because it
concludes with the commandment regarding the making of a
pilgrimage on the three festivals. From the second scroll, the
appropriate passage of the daily offering from Numbers 29 is
read.

The *Haftarah* is from Ezekiel 38 which describes the wars of
Gog and Magog and parallels the prophecy read from Zechariah
on the first day of the festival.

The Torah reading on Shemini Azeret is from Deuteronomy
14:22 through 16:17. This deals with the tithes that the Israelites
were to set aside, with the laws of the Sabbatical year when all
debts were released, and with several statutes requiring generosity
to the poor and the needy. The concluding portion reviews the
three pilgrim festivals: Passover, Shavuot and Sukkot.

This applies to the Diaspora. In Israel, where Shemini Azeret
and Simḥat Torah are the same, the procedure for Simḥat Torah
is followed (see page 102).

From the second scroll, the description of the daily offering
in Numbers 29:35 – 30:1 is read.

The *Haftarah* is from I Kings 8:54-66. The latter part of the
same chapter is read on the second day. It describes Solomon
blessing the people and tells of the 14-day festivities that were
arranged in honor of the Temple's dedication, part of which
coincided with Sukkot.

Yizkor – Memorial Service

It has become customary to hold a brief memorial service for the
dead on Yom Kippur, and on the last day of each of the major
festivals. This memorial service is called *Yizkor* which means "remember," from the opening words of the prayer, *Yizkor*   82

The opening verses of Ecclesiastes from the *Rothschild Siddur* (Italy, 1492).
The superscription reads : "In the afternoon of Simḥat Torah one should
go to the synagogue and recite Ecclesiastes."

Elohim, "May God remember." It is said on Shemini Aẓeret immediately following the reading of the Torah and the *Haftarah*.

Since giving charity has traditionally been regarded as one of the most appropriate ways by which the memory of a deceased is honored, the memorial prayer includes a vow of charity that the person who recites it makes to himself and which he should redeem as soon after the holiday as possible. "Each man shall give as he is able, according to the blessings of the Lord, thy God, which He hath given thee." *Charity*

A mourner still in the year of mourning is not required to recite the *Yizkor* as his grief is still upon him and the memory of the departed has not waned.

There is a widespread custom that those worshipers whose both parents are still alive step outside while the *Yizkor* is recited. There is no halakhic basis for this practice. It may be that it originated with parents who sent their children out during *Yizkor* so as to spare them the sight of the tears and grief that often accompanied the recitation of the memorial prayers.

A *Hoshana* prayer from the *Hamburg Maḥzor* (15th century). The illuminated initial letter *heh* shows a *ḥazzan* holding *aravot*.

84

The Prayer for Rain

Although the entire week of Sukkot is regarded as a judgment period for the year's water supply, and a number of rituals and prayers for water take place during the week, the introduction into the daily *Amidah* of the passage referring to God's power to bring rain — *mashiv ha-ru'ah u-morid ha-gashem* — "Thou causest the wind to blow and the rain to fall" — is delayed until the *Musaf* service of Shemini Azeret. The reason given in the Mishnah for this delay is that rain, if immediately granted, would spoil the holiday rejoicing. In the midst of the festival, rain would not be a blessing, but a curse. It would interfere with the fulfillment of the religious duty to sit in the *sukkah*, and certainly would have dampened the gala Temple festivities for those who came on pilgrimage.

It became customary to accompany the announcement to the congregation that they are to begin to say *mashiv ha-ru'ah* with a special prayer for rain. This is now said with great solemnity at the beginning of the cantor's repetition of the *Musaf Amidah*. In some places, especially in Israel, it is said just prior to the silent recitation of the *Amidah*. The additional passage in the *Amidah* is then said daily till the first day of Passover. When this special prayer for rain is said, the Ark is opened, the cantor dons a white robe as on the High Holy Days, the melody used for the *Kaddish* is the same as that for the *Ne'ilah* service on Yom Kippur. To some degree, it reflects an extension of the judgment theme of the day before.

The central theme that runs through the prayer for rain is *zekhut avot*, "the merit of the fathers." The Jewish people plead for rain and sustenance, claiming not its own worthiness but the righteousness of its saintly ancestors Abraham, Isaac and Jacob. This theme also runs through all of the prayers for forgiveness and atonement on Yom Kippur.

The season chosen for the recitation of this prayer for rain reflects the weather conditions and agricultural needs as they exist in the Land of Israel. Even though for Jews scattered to other parts of the globe this prayer at this time of the year may not be relevant, their continued recitation of this and similar prayers serves to heighten their consciousness of the Holy Land and to help them maintain their spiritual bond with the Land of Israel.

The author of the prayer for rain is Rabbi Eleazar Ha-Kallir who also is the author of the *hoshanot* that are said throughout Sukkot and who was one of the greatest and certainly most prolific of the liturgical poets. He composed *piyyutim*, liturgical poems or poetical prayers for all the festivals and they were widely adopted into the prayer services. Ha-Kallir lived in the Land of Israel probably towards the end of the sixth century although some scholars place him in a later period.

Tefillin on Ḥol ha-Mo'ed

The question of whether or not *tefillin* are put on during the intermediate days of Sukkot has long been a subject of dispute among halakhic authorities. Since all agreed that *tefillin* were not required in the days of the Temple, some authoritative commentaries ruled that *tefillin* are not to be put on during Sukkot. This became the accepted practice for all of Erez Israel as well as among hasidic groups in the Diaspora. The reason is the same as why *tefillin* are not put on on the Sabbath and the festival days themselves. *Tefillin* are to serve as a reminder to the Jew of all the commandments at a time when he is occupied and burdened by everyday concerns. But the Sabbaths and festivals are also called reminders of the Covenant between God and Israel and the sign of God's presence and of His commandments. To add the observance of *tefillin* in the context of its purpose would not only be superfluous but would imply a downgrading of the Sabbath or the festival. The intermediate days too constitute a sufficient *ot*, "sign," particularly on account of the observance of *sukkah* and the Four Species throughout the week (and of

The laws of Sukkot from the *Weill Mahzor* (15th century Italy). The illustrations show various aspects of the festival.

mazzah throughout Passover) and because not all work is permitted.

Other authorities, however, ruled that *tefillin* are put on, and *The Benediction* this remains the practice of most Ashkenazi Jews in the Diaspora. But even among the latter the practice regarding the blessings varies. Some do not recite the blessings at all; others recite them but in a low murmur so as not to require the response of Amen.

In those congregations where *tefillin* are worn, they are worn only through the *Shaharit Amidah*, and are removed before *Hallel*. The remainder of the service is everywhere said without *tefillin*.

The authorities were particularly concerned that this division *Unity* not become a source of conflict in particular synagogues and so insisted that in any given synagogue the same practice prevail; in other words, part of the congregation should not follow one practice while the rest follow the other.

8.   SHEMINI AZERET AND SIMHAT TORAH

Immediately following the seven days of Sukkot, the Torah provides for an additional day of *yom tov*. ". . . On the eighth day you shall observe a sacred occasion, it is a solemn gathering; you shall not work at your occupations." The day is called Shemini Azeret, the Eighth Day of Solemn Assembly and is observed on the 22nd day of Tishrei. In the Diaspora, it is observed for two days, on the 22nd and 23rd of Tishrei. Although this day(s) is commonly regarded as the concluding day(s) of Sukkot, the religious literature and the codes treat it as a festival independent of Sukkot. This is emphasized by the fact that the blessing of *she-heheyanu* ("Blessed art Thou, O Lord our God King of the Universe, Who has kept us alive and sustained us and enabled us to reach this season") is recited when lighting candles and re-

88

Page from the *Rothschild Miscellany*, Italy, c. 1470.
The page contains an illuminated panel of the word
"Hoshana".

Carrying the Scrolls of Law
to the Western Wall on Simḥat
Torah. The Scrolls are carried
under a canopy, *huppah*.

Sukkah decoration, Italy,
c. 1770. Copper engraving,
partly painted. At the bottom
is a depiction of the Feast of
the Drawing of Water. The
engraving is signed at the
bottom left hand corner
(below the figure of Moses)
in Hebrew "Francesco
Griselini, painter."

citing the *Kiddush*. This blessing, reserved for the beginning of a festival, is not said on any of the other days of Sukkot except the first, nor is it said on the concluding day(s) of Passover. Though this day also carries the designation *zeman simḥateinu*, "the season of our rejoicing," none of the special rituals associated with Sukkot are observed on Shemini Aẓeret.

Reasons for the Additional Day

The Bible gives no reason for this additional sacred day. The *Parting is Such* sages looked for one, and based their explanation on the dual *Sweet Sorrow*

"Simḥat Torah," a woodcut by Jacob Steinhardt, 1938.

meaning of the word *azeret*. *Azeret* is translated as assembly, but it also has the meaning of stopping and waiting or of holding back. So they explained it with the following parable: God is like a king who invites all his children to a feast to last for just so many days; when the time comes for them to depart, he says to them: "My children, I have a request to make of you. Stay yet another day; I hate to see you go."

That the sages saw Shemini Azeret in terms of "parting is such sweet sorrow" is typical of their attitude to all the festival days. These were days of joy, not of burden; of pleasure, not only of duty, in which they were guests in the palace of the Lord.

The *Zohar* sees the significance of the day as a way of con- *Universalism* cluding the universalism of Sukkot (see page 23) on a more inti- *and Intimacy* mate note. The parable in the *Zohar* is: "A king invites some guests, and while they are there, all the household attend on them. When they depart, the king says to his household, 'Till now, I and you have been attending to the guests; now I and you will rejoice together for one day.' So God said: 'Up to now, you have been bringing sacrifices for other peoples, now bring one for yourselves.'"

According to some views, however, the purpose of the holi- *The Sukkah on* day was to highlight the stopping (*azeret*) of living in the *sukkah* *Shemini Azeret* so as to mark the conclusion of the festivities in the greater comfort of one's permanent dwelling.

That Shemini Azeret was specifically designated for not sitting in the *sukkah* became the basis of a great dispute among religious authorities, as it related to religious practice in the Diaspora. The controversy centered on the fact that in the Diaspora, the first day of Shemini Azeret is simultaneously regarded as the additional day of Sukkot. If there were no Shemini Azeret, Diaspora Jewry would in any event observe an eighth day as the last day of Sukkot, for an additional day is added in the Diaspora to all the festivals. If one therefore does not sit in the *sukkah* on

90

A *piyyut* for Sukkot from the *Leipzig Maḥzor* (c. 1320). At the bottom the Leviathan and the "wild ox" are depicted.

that day, one in effect nullifies the observance of *sukkah* on what would otherwise be the last day of the holiday. If, on the other hand, one does sit in the *sukkah*, it runs counter to the requirements of the festival of Shemini Aẓeret, whose status is thus reduced. The final decision, which became *halakhah*, is that one should eat in the *sukkah* on the eighth day but should not make the blessing that accompanies it. Nor is one permitted to sleep there, according to most authorities. Only on the ninth day, which is the second day of Shemini Aẓeret, does a Diaspora Jew no longer eat in the *sukkah* either.

Sometime after the 11th century, Shemini Aẓeret also came to be known as Simḥat Torah, "Rejoicing of the Torah." In the Diaspora, this name was applied only to the second day of

Becoming Simḥat Torah

"Simḥat Torah in the Synagogue," a drawing by Bernard Picart, 1724.

Shemini Azeret. Although the name was not known in the talmudic period, the practice of reading the final portion of the
Torah, Deuteronomy 33-34, on this day was set by the Talmud.
From this practice, there gradually grew a tradition of a special
joyous celebration to mark that completion. The basis for such a
celebration is found in the Midrash which described Solomon as *Solomon's*
having made a special feast after he was granted wisdom. Said *Wisdom*
Rabbi Eleazar: "From this we deduce that we make a feast to
mark the conclusion of the Torah, for when God told Solomon 'I
have given you a wise and understanding heart like none who
came before you or after you . . .' and he immediately made a

92

feast for all his servants to celebrate the event, it is only proper to make a feast and celebrate when finishing the Torah."

This is also the basis for the festive meal that is held when *The Siyyum* completing the study of any tractate of the Talmud. The formal completion of a talmudic tractate is called a *siyyum*, which is the Hebrew word for completion. The feast is in the category of a *se'udat mitzvah*, a meal of religious significance. Since a *se'udat mitzvah* takes precedence over the fast of the firstborn on the eve of Passover, and over the prohibition of eating meat during the Nine Days (the period prior to Tishah be-Av), a *siyyum* is sometimes planned for those occasions to gain a dispensation from those prohibitions.

While the tradition of added merriment on this last day of *The Name* the holiday in honor of completing the Torah began during the ninth and tenth centuries of the common era, at the time of the Geonim, the name Simḥat Torah came into use even later. And while the reading of the last portion of the Torah was set by the Talmud, the reading of the first chapter of Genesis was not introduced on Simḥat Torah until sometime after the 12th century. The reasons given for this additional reading were: 1) to indicate that "just as we were privileged to witness its completion, so shall we be privileged to witness its beginning" and 2) to prevent Satan from accusing Israel that they were happy to finish the Torah (in the sense of getting it over with) and did not care to continue to read it.

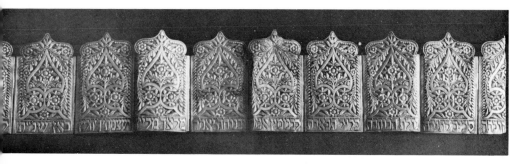

A distinctive silver headpiece (or belt) for the Torah scroll.
Rhodes, unknown date.

Initially it was the custom for the same person who com- pleted Deuteronomy to read the Genesis portion from memory without using a scroll, on account of the general rule that "two scrolls are not taken out for one reader." Eventually the practice developed of calling two different persons, one for the reading of the last portion of Deuteronomy and one for the first portion of Genesis, and two different scrolls began to be used. Each of these *aliyot* came to be regarded as great honors. The people so honored were called *Ḥatanim*, bridegrooms. The one who presided over the completion of Deuteronomy was called *Ḥatan Torah*, Bridegroom of the Torah. The one who presided over the beginning of Genesis was called *Ḥatan Bereshit*, the Bridegroom of Genesis. It became customary for the men so honored to sponsor a festive meal later in the day. In our own day, those so honored usually sponsor a special *Kiddush* following the services.

Although the day is now commonly known as Simḥat Torah, the prayers and the *Kiddush* of the day still refer to it as Shemini Azeret.

Hakkafot

The ritual custom most closely identified with Simḥat Torah is that of the *hakkafot*. *Hakkafot* is the term used to designate ceremonial processional circuits, whether in the synagogue or elsewhere. On Simḥat Torah, all the Torah scrolls are removed from the Ark, and carried around the *bimah* in seven *hakkafot*. This takes place during the evening service and also during the morning service. Ḥasidic practice in the Diaspora is to conduct *hakkafot* also at the evening service of the first day of Shemini Azeret.

Although the custom of *hakkafot* on Simḥat Torah is of rather late origin, dating from about the last third of the 16th century (in the city of Safed), the practice of *hakkafot* goes back much further. Processional circuits are first mentioned in the Bible, as a build-up to the downfall of the walls of Jericho. There

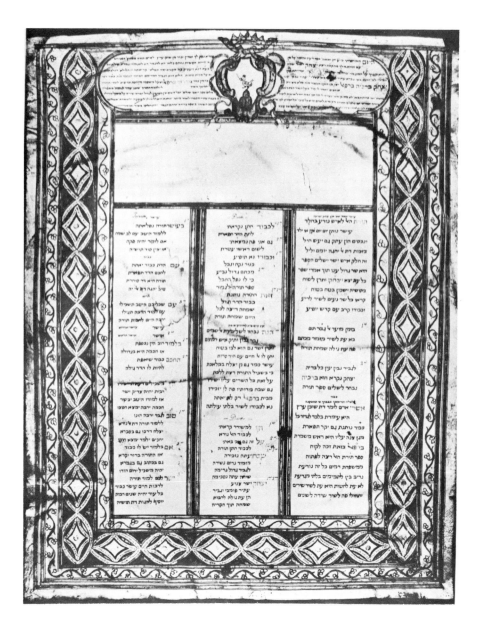

Illuminated scroll from Rome with the text of a cantata celebrating the appointment of Isaac Berechiah Baraffael as *Ḥatan Torah*, 1766.

Simḥat Torah *hakkafot* in Tel Aviv, 1965.

were seven circuits around Jericho; once a day for six days, and seven times on the seventh day. The *lulav* (and *aravot* too) were carried around the Temple altar during the seven days of Sukkot; once a day during the first six days, and seven times on the seventh day. From there developed the custom of *hakkafot* around the synagogue with the *lulav* and *etrog*.

At traditional Jewish wedding ceremonies the custom of *hakkafot* is still to be seen in the circling by the bride around the bridegroom at the very start of the ceremony. Three such circuits can be said to symbolize the three-part passage from the Prophets

At Weddings

96

The procession to the Western Wall, 1970. Chief Rabbi Nissim is under the *tallit* spread in the manner of a marriage canopy.

which describes Israel's relationship to God in terms of an idyllic betrothal and marriage:

I will betroth you unto me forever;
I will betroth you unto me in righteousness and judgment, in lovingkindness and mercy;
I will betroth you unto me in faithfulness and you shall know the Lord.

By circling, the bride symbolizes her desire to surround her husband with the qualities that the Prophet describes as the essence of a fulfilling and enduring marriage. These same verses are said every weekday morning by the adult male Jew when he puts on the *tefillin*.

Seven circuits are generally commemorative of Joshua's march around Jericho. However, the juxtaposition of the "circle" with the mystical figure seven possessed special meaning in magical rites as well as in kabbalistic traditions.

Although the prescribed number of *hakkafot* is not indicated *The Number* in the *Shulḥan Arukh*, and religious authorities are quoted as saying that *hakkafot* are done three times or seven times, "each according to his custom," the custom of seven *hakkafot* has become universally adopted in our times. The popularity of the *hakkafot* is probably due to the fact that most everyone, including the children, are given an opportunity to participate.

All the Torah scrolls are removed from the Ark, and while *The Ritual* one is held by the reader, all the others are divided among the worshipers. The reader leads the procession around the synagogue, chanting passages with the refrain:

> *Ana Adonai hoshi'ah na*
> *Ana Adonai haẓliḥah na*

which means, "Please, O Lord, save us; Please, O Lord, make us succeed." After each circuit, the scrolls are handed to others, so as to accord the honor to as many people as possible. Small children are generally given decorative flags or miniature scrolls and they too follow the Torah scrolls in the processions. In addition to the prescribed passages, it is commonplace for the congregation to join in the singing of many additional songs, generally verses from the Bible or the prayerbook that have been put to music.

It is also the practice in the more traditional congregations for the worshipers to join a circle and dance in between each circuit. Those holding Torah scrolls also join the dancing.

In the yeshivot, the schools of higher Jewish learning, and in *To the Heights* those congregations where traditional youth predominates, the *of Ecstasy* singing and dancing that accompany the *hakkafot* can last for

Hakkafot in the Yoḥanan Ben Zakkai synagogue in the Jewish quarter of Jerusalem's Old City. This historic synagogue was totally destroyed during the Jordanian occupation. It was rebuilt after 1967.

99

many hours. It is sometimes even carried outdoors. The whirling bodies and the stomping feet, perhaps a performance of acrobatic feats by someone inside the dancing circle, all accompanied by continuous song, provides a scene of ecstatic joy.

Torah scrolls being carried under a *huppah* (marriage canopy) in the plaza at the Western Wall. This took place during *hol ha-mo'ed* Sukkot 1972 at the annual pilgrimage to Jerusalem.

In Jerusalem, it is now customary on Simḥat Torah morning for some congregations to join together in a mass dancing procession through the city to the Western Wall. Led by scrolls of the Torah carried under canopies, literally thousands of people, young and old, eight and ten abreast, dance and sing their way to

To the Western Wall

the Western Wall in a procession that stretches for as far as the eye can see.

The talmudic description of the *Simḥat Bet ha-Sho'eva* as a scene which if "one has not seen . . . has not witnessed joy in his

Distributing sweetmeats to the children on Simḥat Torah; a 17th-century woodcut.

life" can aptly be applied to many of the Simḥat Torah celebrations in our own day.

In past centuries, lighted torches were carried by men during *Candles in* the *hakkafot*. This custom came down to this century in the *Apples* form of lighted candles placed into apples implanted on the flags that older children carried in the procession. Today's adult generation still remembers this. As congregations became more sensitive to the danger of fire the practice waned.

The original custom of holding the *hakkafot* at the conclusion of Simḥat Torah inspired the custom in Israel of carrying the Simḥat Torah celebration also into the night after the holiday. Public gatherings with bands and music featuring *hakkafot* and singing and dancing are then held. In one public square of Jerusalem, it is customary for the Chief Rabbis and high government officials to participate. At that celebration there is featured the varied practices of the different Jewish communities: Ḥasidic, Yemenite, Bukharan, native Israeli, etc. A different group is responsible for each of the *hakkafot*, doing it in their respective traditional dress and with their traditional melodies. *Hakkafot* also take place at Israel's army bases, and even men near frontline positions have been known to participate in them during quiet periods. In the midst of the Yom Kippur War which lasted till after Sukkot, television crews recorded scenes of the Chief Rabbi of Israel, Shlomo Goren, visiting forward army bases, having brought with him a small Torah scroll, and of men joining him in some traditional dancing with the Torah.

Aliyot for Everyone

The next most distinctive feature of the Simḥat Torah ritual is the custom of calling to the Torah every adult male worshiper. To make this possible, the reading from the beginning of the *sidra*, Deuteronomy 33:1, through verse 26, is repeated as many times as necessary in order to accommodate everyone present. In some places, the congregation separates into smaller groups, with some going into side rooms for the Torah reading, so as to minimize the time needed in giving everyone an *aliyah*.

Having done all this, the *Ḥatan Torah* is then called up for the final verses in Deuteronomy, 33:27 — 34:12. His calling up is preceded by a rather lengthy proclamation, a special liturgical composition called *Me-reshut ha-El ha-gadol*, "By permission of the great God," and read in the fashion of a royal proclamation. As the last sentence of Deuteronomy is concluded, the congregation rises and calls out: *Ḥazak Ḥazak Venithazek*, "Be strong, be strong, and let us be strengthened." This declaration is made not only on this occasion, but whenever any one of the Five Books of Moses is completed.

When the first Torah is lifted up for the purpose of dressing it, the congregation recites the passage: "And this is the Torah that Moses placed before the Children of Israel, by the command of the Lord, by the hand of Moses."

Sephardi Jews have a custom to lift their right hands and with their small fingers outstretched, point in the direction of the Torah when saying this passage. In Israel, this practice is spreading among young Ashkenazi Jews as well.

The second scroll is then opened to Genesis and the *Ḥatan Bereshit* is called up for the reading which consists of Genesis 1:1 – 2:31. For him too, a similar proclamation is first read, called *Me-reshut Meromam*, "By permission of the One On High."

Bukharan Jews in Tel Aviv don their traditional costumes for the Second *Hakkafot*. Rabbi Yiẓhak Yedidyah Fraenkel, the present Chief Rabbi of Tel Aviv, is in the center.

The final *aliyah* is that of the *Maftir*. In addition to the Torah passage (Numbers 29:35—30:1) this person also reads the *Haftarah* for the day.

In addition to involving the children in the Torah procession, it also became customary to include them in the Torah reading. Although a child under the age of thirteen is not generally called to the Torah for an *aliyah*, on Simḥat Torah there developed the custom of *kol ha-ne'arim* which means "all the children," and refers to the fact that all of the children in the congregation are called up collectively and given a joint *aliyah*. A *tallit* is spread over the heads of the entire group and the blessings, led by one adult, are recited. At the conclusion of the reading, the congregation invokes Jacob's blessing of Ephraim and Manasseh as a special blessing for the children.

> May the Angel who has redeemed me from all harm, bless the children. In them may my name be recalled, and the names of my fathers, Abraham and Isaac . . . .

Custom differs as to what point in the Torah reading this collective *aliyah* is given to the children. Most congregations arrange this *aliyah* just prior to that of the *Ḥatan Torah*. Some have the practice of calling *kol ha-ne'arim* together with the *Ḥatan Torah*; others do so together with the *Ḥatan Bereshit*.

In some places it is also customary to have a short Torah reading from the concluding portion of Deuteronomy read on Simḥat Torah night, when three persons are called up. Where this is done, it is the only time in the year when the Torah scroll is read in the synagogue at night. In some places the evening reading was reserved for special selections containing such biblical blessings as from Genesis 27:28 and from Genesis 48:16. It became customary around the 16th century for people to "bid" for these *aliyot* by vowing money to charity to receive the privilege, and so these Torah passages came to be called *nedarim* (vows).

The *Ushpizin* prayer in the form of a *sukkah* decoration. *Ushpizin* (Aramaic for "guests) is an invitation to the souls of Abraham, Isaac, Jacob, Joseph, Moses, Aaron and David to enter the *sukkah*. Moses and Aaron are depicted in this decoration. Germany, 18th century, parchment.

Ushpizin plaque for the *sukkah* with depictions
of the "invited guests." Abraham is depicted
by a house with many doors open to all visitors,
Isaac by the sacrifice scene, Jacob by his dream of
angels ascending and descending the heavenly ladder,
Moses as the giver of the Law, Aaron performing
priestly functions, Joseph as the seer and interpreter
of dreams, and David as a musician. "Underglass
painting," Rumania, 19th century.

This Simḥat Torah custom seems to have been the origin of a practice still prevailing in some synagogues of offering *aliyot* for sale on such special occasions as the High Holy Days, or of asking for vows of charity, from those receiving *aliyot*. A special blessing for them (*mi-she-beirakh*) is also recited afterwards.

In contemporary synagogues of more progressive inclinations, the practice of *nedarim* was eliminated. As these contributions came to be looked upon as "a payment" for receiving an *aliyah*, the practice came to be regarded as gross. Furthermore, it served to limit these honors to the rich who could give greater sums, and this ran counter to the emerging sense of democracy and equality that became manifest in the community. And so other means for raising the funds to sustain the synagogues and the schools of learning were resorted to. But as a free-will offering, the principle of sending in a contribution to maintain the synagogue or Jewish schools of learning in gratitude and appreciation for receiving an honor remains sound. *Modern Practice*

Kiddush on Simḥat Torah

Generally *Kiddush* is recited on Sabbath and festival mornings following the conclusion of the services. On Simḥat Torah, however, particularly in the Diaspora, *Kiddush* has taken a somewhat different form. The tables are laid with wine, drinks and baked goods in outer rooms and as individuals complete their *aliyah*, they proceed to make *Kiddush* and partake of refreshments although the services are far from over. The atmosphere is one of frivolity which in some instances, unfortunately, degenerates into a loss of decorum even within the synagogue. The general frivolity includes pranks performed by the children in tying the fringes of people's *tallitot* to banisters or to one another.

In many places, young people spend the rest of the day visiting each other's homes, being treated to refreshments at each place.

The right of every Jew to rejoice in Torah and to celebrate on

Dancing with the Torah scrolls at the termination of Simḥat Torah in Kefar Ḥabad, Israel. The celebrations there have become a national event.

Simḥat Torah, even though one is not learned in it nor regularly studies it, is affirmed in a hasidic tale. A Rebbe once saw a simple and ignorant wagon driver singing and dancing on Simḥat Torah. He said to him, "What does all the joy mean to you anyway? Do you then claim a share in the study of Torah all the rest of the year?" "Rebbe," answered the wagon driver, "if a brother of mine has a *simḥah*, am I not permitted to rejoice? Isn't his *simḥah* also mine?"

My Brother's Simḥah

The Triennial Cycle

The celebration of Simḥat Torah had its origin in Babylonia and was based on the practice of reading and completing the entire Five Books of Moses in the synagogue during the course of a single year. The Five Books were divided into 54 portions (*sedarim*) which is the number of Sabbaths in a leap year. In ancient Palestine, however, cycles of three and three and a half years to complete the entire Torah were followed. The reading was consecutive and based on a division which numbered either 154 or 175 Sedarim. Each of the 154 *sedarim* also had its own

106

corresponding selection from the Prophets (*Haftarah*). The so-called "triennial cycle" introduced by some contemporary congregations in order to abbreviate the Torah reading each Sabbath does not at all correspond to the ancient system. The contemporary innovation consists of reading only a third of each weekly *sidra* of the annual cycle. The reading is not consecutive over a three year period.

In the triennial cycle, the readings from the Prophets were *The Haftarah* also arranged so that each *Haftarah* was said only once in three years, rather than once a year. The chapters from the Prophets were selected on the basis of a relationship to the Torah passages read on that day, or to the special observance of the day. Different *Haftarot* were chosen on each of the three years, even for the special occasions. So that for Sukkot for example, on the first year of the cycle, when Genesis 32 was read, the *Haftarah* was Zechariah 14:16-19; for the second year when Leviticus 9:10 was read, the *Haftarah* was I Kings 8:8; and for the third year when Deuteronomy 8:9 was read, the *Haftarah* was Isaiah 4:6.

The triennial cycle was so designed that the beginning of certain portions coincided with the different New Years: thus Genesis was begun on the first of Nisan (the ecclesiastical New Year); Deuteronomy on the first of Elul; Leviticus on the first of Tishrei; and Exodus and Numbers on the fifteenth of Shevat. These dates mark the four New Years enumerated in the Mishnah. As the Jews of Palestine did not have an annual completion of the Torah, they did not have an annual Torah completion celebration. Theirs was held every three or three and a half years.

The transition from the triennial to the annual reading even *The Transition* in Palestine took place sometime after the 12th century. The transference of the beginning of the cycle, i.e., Genesis, from Nisan to Tishrei may have been due to the smallness of the *sedarim* under the old system and to the fact that people were thus only reminded of the chief festivals once in three years. It was therefore arranged that Deuteronomy 28 should fall just before the New Year, so that the beginning of the cycle should always come immediately after the Sukkot festival.

It is interesting to note that in about 174 c.e., one of the *Evidence from a* Church fathers, Chrysostom, declared that it was customary to *Church Father* begin reading from Genesis during Lent, which corresponds with Nisan. Thus it seems that, till the end of the second century, the Church followed the Palestine synagogues in commencing the reading of the Bible at the beginning of the Jewish ecclesiastical New Year.

The Awakening of Russian Jewry

One of the truly miraculous developments in the spiritual odyssey of the Jewish people in the 20th century was the sudden re-awakening of Jewish self-awareness in Russia. Only a few short years ago, in the middle 1960s, Elie Wiesel described Russian Jewry as "The Jews of Silence," whose eyes were filled with fear and anguish. This was the older generation. As for the younger generation, they were nowhere to be seen. After half a century of Communist rule, where religious instruction and Jewish education could not officially take place, where Jewish culture was suppressed, and where the traditions of Judaism were difficult, if not impossible, to keep, the assimilated status of the young Russian Jew posed no surprise.

Yet seemingly out of nowhere, and despite the dangers involved, small groups of young Russian Jews gathered one Simḥat Torah eve around the synagogues in Moscow and Leningrad. There they sang Hebrew songs and danced the traditional Jewish folk dances, just as was being done that night in synagogues elsewhere in the world. Word of the gatherings spread and it was repeated again and again during the following years. The numbers of participants swelled to tens of thousands and the practice spread to other cities. Young people streamed to the vicinity of the synagogue on Simḥat Torah eve to affirm their Jewish selves;

A Simḥat Torah scene in the Moscow synagogue in 1969. Some
women have joined the men on the main floor to watch the *hakkafot*.

to express their solidarity with the State of Israel and the Jewish
people everywhere.

Although these were all people whose religious training was
nil, and what was emerging was a nationalistic feeling of people-
hood and heritage, it is significant that this feeling found its
expression not only around one of the religious festivals, but
more specifically around the one holiday that more than any
other highlights the centrality of Torah in Jewish life and joy-
ously celebrates it, not as a commemoration of a past event, but
as an expression of contemporary relevance and meaning. Once
again there was dramatic evidence — to paraphrase a famous dic-
tum on the Sabbath — that even more than Israel has kept the
Torah, the Torah has kept Israel.

Kiddush in the *sukkah* by Moritz Oppenheim. The maid is waiting
to bring in the soup and two non-Jewish schoolboys are intrigued.

Amidah, main prayer recited at all services while standing; also known as *Shemoneh esreh*.

Ashkenazi (plural Ashkenazim), German or West-, Central-, or East-European Jew(s), as contrasted with Sephardi.

Bet Din, rabbinic court of law.

Geonim, heads of the academies in post-talmudic period, especially in Babylonia.

Halakhah, the overall term for Jewish law; also the accepted authoritative decision on any specific question.

Ḥanukkah, eight-day celebration starting the twenty-fifth day of the month of Kislev (usually falls in December), commemorating the Hasmonean victory led by Judah Maccabee over the Syrian king Antiochus Epiphanes and the subsequent re-dedication of the Temple.

Ḥasid (plural Ḥasidim), adherents of religious movement founded in first half of the 18th century.

Ḥazzan, one who leads the prayers in the synagogue. Also called *sheliaḥ zibbur*.

Kiddush, prayer of sanctification recited on Sabbath and festivals; it is said over wine or bread.

Midrash, collection of rabbinic interpretations of, and homilies on, the Bible.

Mishnah, earliest codification of the Oral Law, completed in the third century c.e.

Mitzvah (plural *Mitzvot*), biblical or rabbinic injunction; applied also to good deeds.

Nisan, the Spring month when Passover is observed; it is reckoned as the first month of the ecclesiastical year, the seventh month of the civil year.

Passover, the first of the three pilgrim festivals, commemorating the Exodus from Egypt, observed for seven days in Israel, eight days in the Diaspora.

Piyyut (plural *Piyyutim*), liturgical poems. Many were incorporated into the festival services.

Rosh Ha-Shanah, the New Year, which is also the start of the ten-day period of repentance, observed for two days in Israel and in the Diaspora.

Sephardi (plural Sephardim), Jew(s) of Spain and Portugal and their descendants. Contrasted with Ashkenazi.

Shavuot, the second of the three pilgrim festivals, commemorating the giving of the Ten Commandments at Mount Sinai, observed for one day in Israel, two days in the Diaspora.

Sidra (plural *sedarim* or *sidrot*), that portion of the Torah read each week on the Sabbath.

Talmud, compendium of discussions on the Mishnah by generations of scholars in many academies over a period of several centuries; consists of *halakhah* and *aggadah.*

Tishrei, the month in which the High Holy Days fall; it is reckoned as the first month of the civil calendar, and the seventh month of the ecclesiastical year.

Yom Kippur, the Day of Atonement, a day for repentance and fasting observed on the tenth day of Tishrei, five days before Sukkot.

113

ABBREVIATIONS TO SOURCES

BIBLE

Gen.	– Genesis	Jud.	– Judges	Ps.	– Psalms
Ex.	– Exodus	Sam.	– Samuel	Songs	– Song of Songs
Lev.	– Leviticus	Is.	– Isaiah	Ecc.	– Ecclesiastes
Num.	– Numbers	Ezek.	– Ezekiel	Neh.	– Nehemiah
Deut.	– Deuteronomy	Hos.	– Hosea	Chron.	– Chronicles
		Zech.	– Zechariah		

TALMUD[1]

TJ	– Jerusalem Talmud[2]				
Ar.	– *Arakhin*	Hul.	– *Ḥullin*	Pes.	– *Pesaḥim*
Av.Z.	– *Avodah Zara*	Kal.	– *Kallah*	RH	– *Rosh ha-Shanah*
Ber.	– *Berakhot*	Ket.	– *Ketubbot*	Shab.	– *Shabbat*
BK	– *Bava Kamma*	Meg.	– *Megillah*	Suk.	– *Sukkah*
Der. Er.	– *Derekh Ereẓ*	Mk	– *Mo'ed Katan*	Ta'an.	– *Ta'anit*

LATER AUTHORITIES

Yad	– Maimonides, *Yad ha-Ḥazakah*
Tur, OH	– *Tur Shulḥan Arukh, Oraḥ Ḥayyim*
Sh. Ar.	– *Shulḥan Arukh*
OH	– *Oraḥ Ḥayyim*
YD	– *Yoreh De'ah*

[1] References to the Mishnah are in the form Suk. 1:1 (i.e., Tractate *Sukkah*, chapter 1, Mishnah 1); references to the Gemara are in the form: Suk. 10a (i.e., Tractate *Sukkah*, page 10, first side).

[2] Otherwise all Talmud references are to the Babylonian Talmud.

SOURCES

page

1   "The Lord spoke to Moses . . ." – Lev. 23:33–34

1   "Three times a year . . ." – Deut. 16:16

2   "The first day . . ." – Lev. 23:35

2   On the first day . . . Ex. 12:16

2   in biblical . . . sources – Num. 29:12; Deut. 16:14; I Kings 8:2, 65; 12:32; Ezek. 45:25; Neh. 8:14,18; II Chron. 5:3, 7:8.

3   "at the end of the year" – Ex. 23:16

4   "You shall live in booths . . ." –Lev. 23:42–43

4   as a protection against the sun – Rashi to Suk. 11b

5   "clouds of glory" – Suk. 11b

5   "God linked with Israel . . ." – *Zohar, Emor* 103a

6   these "clouds" that provided protection – Tur, OH 625

6   elsewhere in the Bible too – Is. 4:5,6; II Sam. 22:12; Job 36:29; Ps. 18:12

6   various rational explanations – *Encyclopaedia Judaica* 13:524

7   To reverse the normal practice – Tur, OH 625

7   "For in the day of trouble . . ." – Ps. 27:5

7   the fragile *sukkah* as a symbol of poverty – Philo, Laws, Book 2: 208; Maimonides, *Guide to the Perplexed* 3:43

8   "the levite, the stranger . . ." – Deut. 16:14

8   "whoever abides under the shadow of faith . . ." – *Zohar, Emor* 103a

8   three kinds of servitude . . . three types of freedom – S. Goren, *Torat Ha-Moadim*, p. 113

9   the "Feast of Ingathering" – Ex. 23:16; 34:22

9   "at the end of the year..." – Deut. 16:13

10   at this time of the year – Maimonides, *Guide to the Perplexed* 3:43

10   "filled with the ingathered crops . . ." – Rashbam to Ex. 23:16

11   in terms of Israel's ingratitude – Is. 1:2

11   she said "This time I will thank . . ." – Gen. 29:35

11   "It is a good thing . . ." – Ps. 92:2

11   "Four are required to give thanks . . ." – Ber. 54b

13   "Were our mouths full of song . . ." – Prayerbook, *Nishmat* prayer

14   it is mentioned three times – Lev. 23:40; Deut. 16:14; Deut. 16:15

14   "because you did not serve . . ." – Deut. 28:47

115

page

14   "Serve the Lord with gladness . . ." – Ps. 100:2

14   Let the righteous be glad . . . – Ps. 68:4

15   reflected . . . in song – Ar. 11

15   The *Shekhinah* rests . . . – Pes. 117a

15   it is proper to dance before the bride – Ket. 16b; Kal. 10; Der. Er. 6

16   "When the month of Adar enters . . ." – *Magen Avraham* to Sh. Ar., OH 686, n.5

16   "One rejoicing may not be merged . . ." – MK 8b

16   requesting the peace of Jerusalem – Ps. 122:6

16   "Rejoice with Jerusalem . . ." – Is. 66:10

16   "If I set not Jerusalem above . . ." – Ps. 137:6

16   "The joy of the whole earth . . ." – Ps. 48:3

16   sadness . . .regarded as sacreligious – *Midrash Rabba, Pekudai* 52:4

16   "there is no rejoicing except . . ." – MK 9a

19   was described by the noted author – The Jerusalem Post, October 12, 1973

19   the same significance in the Four Species – Munk, *The World of Prayer*, vol. II, p. 275

20   the world is judged at four periods – RH 1:1

20   the theme reflected in the waving ritual – *Sefer Ravyah* 683

20   man's fate is also sealed – Tur. OH 664

21   "the day of the aravah is . . ." – *Shibolei Haleket* 121

21   "In that day will I raise up . . ." – Amos 9:11

22   "All who fulfill . . ." – *Yalkut Shimoni, Emor* 653

22   Sodom . . . rehabilitated – Ezek. 16:55; *Midrash Tanhuma,* Buber (ed.), p. 16

22   the biblical commandment to build – Deut. 27:5

23   one poem describes a father – Shimon Prog, Yiddish folk song

24   "it shall come to pass that every one . . ." – Zech. 14:16

24   "the test that will be given . . ." – Av. Z. 3a

24   "To what do the seventy bulls correspond?" – Suk. 55b

25   "All who fulfill . . ." – *Yalkut Shimoni, Emor* 653

25   *behemoth* – Job 40:15

25   says Samson Raphael Hirsch – *Be-Ma'aglei Shanah*, vol. 1, p. 143

25   the verse from Isaiah – Is. 27:1

27   "And all the congregation . . ." – Neh. 8:17

27   "Go forth unto the mount . . ." – Neh. 15

29   patterned after Sukkot – II Maccabees 1,10

29   two halakhic disputes – Shab. 21a; BK 62b; TJ BK 6;7

page

31   the Four Species together with circumcision – *Mekhilta devei Rabbi Yishmael, Yitro*

32   Sukkot in New Testament – John 7:37; Mark 9:2

32   they pelted him with their *etrogim* – Suk. 4:9

34   The Mishnah records – Suk. 4:4

34   Adults would grab *lulavim* – Suk. 4:7

37   A fourteenth-century source . . . – M. Ha-Kohen in *Maḥanayim*, vol. 61 (1962), p. 32–33

38   "Every seventh year . . ." – Deut. 31:10–12

39   blowing of trumpets – Yad, Ḥagigah 3:7

40   Jordan Valley area of Israel – Gen. 33:17; II Sam. 1:11; I Kings 20:12

40   Throughout the seven days – Suk. 2:9

43   "When a man sits . . ." – *Zohar, Emor* 103b

43   "Enter, enter, exalted holy guests . . ." – *Zohar, Emor* 103b

44   Rules of Construction – Sh. Ar., OH 628–635

44   The sages pointed to the relationship . . . – Rashi to Suk. 1a

48   No blessing is said – Sh. Ar., OH 641:1

49   Decoration of the *sukkah* – *Tosefta* Suk. 1

49   immediately after Yom Kippur – Rema to Sh. Ar., OH 625:1

50   "So the people went forth . . ." – Neh. 8:16–18

50   "On the first day you shall take . . ." – Lev. 23:40

54   "That these four were chosen . . ." – Maimonides, *Guide to the Perplexed* 3:43

55   The Midrash explains – Lev. R. 30:9–12

57   the sages also called for waving it – Yad, Lulav 7:9

58   in commemoration of the Temple – Suk. 3:12

60   "Then shall the trees . . ." – I Chron. 16:33

60   as a rite by which "evil winds" – Suk. 37b

68   "laws given to Moses at Sinai" – Suk. 44a, Ta'an.3a

69   The Talmud describes the ritual – Suk. 45a

71   When Samuel was about to pray – I Sam. 7:6

71   When David's three friends – II Sam. 23:16

71   Gideon, wishing to make a sacrifice – Jud. 6:19

71   four pitchers of water that Elijah – I Kings 18:34

71   The water for the ritual was drawn – Hul. 48a

72   The vessel used – Suk. 48a

72   "with joy shall you draw water . . ." – Is. 12:3

72   "One who has not seen the rejoicing . . ." – Suk. 50a

72   Rabbi Simeon ben Gamaliel . . .would juggle – Suk. 53a

77   the subject of great rabbinic controversy – Shab. 30b

77   "Vanity of vanities . . ." – Ecc. 1:2

77   "There is nothing new . . ." – Ecc. 1:9

77   "To everything there is a season . . ." – Ecc. 3:1

77   "As he came forth . . ." – Ecc. 5:14

77   "A good name is better . . ." – Ecc. 7:1

78   "The end of the matter . . ." – Ecc. 12:13

84   Each man shall give as he is able – Deut. 16:17

85   The reason given is the Mishnah – Ta'an. 1:1

88   ". . . on the eighth day . . ." – Lev. 23:36

90   God is like a king – Rashi to Lev. 23:36

90   The parable in the *Zohar* – *Zohar, Emor* 104b

92   the practice . . . was set by the Talmud – Meg. 31a

92   Said Rabbi Eleazar, "From this we deduce . . ." – Songs.R.1

93   This is also the basis for the festive meal – *Biur Hagra* to Sh. Ar., YD 246:76

93   "just as we were privileged . . ." – Abudraham, *Hamanhig* 55

93   to prevent Satan – Tur, OH 669; *Sifri*, Deut. 33

94   "two scrolls are not taken out . . ." – *Shibolei Haleket* 372

97   "I will betroth you unto me . . ." – Hos. 2:21–22

98   religious authorities are quoted – *Mishnah Brurah* to Sh. Ar., OH 669, n.10

104   "The angel who has redeemed . . ." – Gen. 48:16

107   the four New Years enumerated in the Mishnah – RH 1:1

READING LIST

Encyclopaedia Judaica, Jerusalem, 1972, under: *Etrog,* Four Species, *Hakhel,* Hoshana
Rabbah, *Lulav,* Simhat Torah, *Sukkah,* Sukkot.

Donin, Hayim Halevy, *To Be a Jew,* New York, 1972.
Fabricant, Isaac N., *A Guide to Succoth,* London, 1958.
Goodman, Philip, *The Sukkot Anthology,* Philadelphia, 1963.
Munk, Elie, *The World of Prayer,* New York, 1963.
Vainstein, Yaacov, *The Cycle of the Jewish Year,* Israel, 1964.